POETRY MATTERS

Edited by Mark Richardson

Northern Poets

First published in Great Britain in 2011 by:

 Young**Writers**

Remus House
Coltsfoot Drive
Peterborough
PE2 9BF
Telephone: 01733 890066
Website: www.youngwriters.co.uk

Foreword

Since our inception in 1991, Young Writers has endeavoured to promote poetry and creative writing within schools by running annual nationwide competitions. These competitions are designed to develop and nurture the burgeoning creativity of the next generation, and give them valuable confidence in their own abilities.

This regional anthology is one of the series produced by our latest secondary school competition, *Poetry Matters*. Using poetry as their tool, the young writers were given the opportunity to tell the world what matters to them. The authors of our favourite three poems were also given the chance to appear on the front cover of their region's collection.

Whilst skilfully conveying their opinions through poetry, the writers showcased in this collection have simultaneously managed to give poetry a breath of fresh air, brought it to life and made it relevant to them. Using a variety of themes and styles, our featured poets leave a lasting impression of their inner thoughts and feelings, making this anthology a rare insight into the next generation.

Contents

The Poems

T24s Tour Of Reach

So let's take a trip to a planet called Reach,
It's a planet of war, but we like to chill on the beach.

Right here it goes Spartans vs Elites,
Elites aren't all of them, but some burst into sweets!

I'm not going to bore you with the story, mainly 'cause of spoilers,
So we'll head to multiplayer where the action tends to boil first.

Join up with my friends, we're gonna play some team SWAT,
Basic rules of the playlist is to get 'em with a head shot!

Doesn't matter if you win or lose, it's how you play the game,
The best part is you always get some credits at the end.

Let's hop on to invasion, where it's grab the core and run,
Watch out for the snipers scratching tallies on their guns.

Now let's jump to team objective to play some CTF,
Wow, these guys are terrible, are there any good players left?

And now it's tangent time! Let's play about in game chat,
Talking about some random stuff before a vehicle - oh snap!

Whoa, I love this map, let's go battle-bro, armour lock,
One last kill to win with only twenty seconds on the clock!

Ha! I love the hologram, such a neat little trick,
The reaction is so priceless when a player falls for it.

So there's my adventures from the sunny planet Reach,
It was all great fun, but now I'm dead on that beach.

Peter Vicars
Academy 360, Sunderland

Cats

A fat cat
A thin cat
A brown cat
A black cat.
Cats on the wall
Cats on the gate
Cats on the window
Cats on the ceiling.
A blue cat
A yellow cat
A long cat
A short cat.

A mew cat
A miaow cat
A scratch cat
A hiss cat.
Cats in the bin
Cats in the telly
Cats in your pen.
A fluffy cat
A scary cat
A cuddly cat
A random cat.

A white cat
A green cat
An old cat
A young cat.
Cats on the computer
Cats in the kitchen.
Cats on the roof
Cats on the car
Cats in the sky.

Kitten cats
Small cats
Big cats
Candy cats
Cats . . .

Shaun Hunt (14)
Academy 360, Sunderland

My Little Sister

My little sister
Is totally insane
Banging on doors
And then complains!

My little sister
Couldn't clean a floor
It's always dirty
Like a big cave door.

My little sister
Is always a pain
So please do me a favour
And take her to Spain.

My little sister
Has these silly pencils
Once I caught them
Dancing with stencils.

My little sister
Is as pale as snow
She came in yesterday
Her temperature was low.

My little sister
Was late for school
Crying loudly
In a swimming pool.

Brogan Henson (11)
Academy 360, Sunderland

My Family

I love being in my family.
This is where I want to be.
My mam always makes me a lovely tea,
So it makes me smile with glee.
My family is what matters to me.

My mam and dad,
Help me when I'm sad.
I even love my brother when he's raging mad.
My sister also has a boyfriend called Brad,
My family is what matters to me.

Me, me, me.
I am Ellie.
I love blue jelly,
That goes in my belly.
My family is what matters to me.

Bruno, Bruno is my dog,
He really grunts like a hog.
He is even scared of a little green frog.
My family is what matters to me.

So let's leave it at that,
So give yourself a pat.
You tried hard, you done good!
Well, now I must go and eat some yummy food!
My family is what matters to me.

Ellie Rodwell (11)
Academy 360, Sunderland

My Family

My brothers are what matters to me,
I have two brothers,
I wouldn't wish for any others.
They are older than me,
Them I always like to see,
My brothers are what matter to me.

My dad is what matters to me,
My dad is quite funny.
He loves eating honey,
My dad loves his beer
And he once ran over a deer.
My dad is what matters to me.

My mum is what matters to me,
My mum can cook
And read a book.
My mum is very kind,
I hope she will never go blind,
My mum is what matters to me.

Family is what matters to me,
My family may be small,
My family may be tall.
We stick together through thick and thin,
We never hit each other with a rolling pin,
Family is what matters to me.

Reece Emms (11)
Academy 360, Sunderland

Personally . . .

Music is everything, a stage and a mic,
But in this world there's a lot I don't like!

N-Dubz can rap and all that,
But to be honest, they sound like a cat!

Scooter enjoys his little hum,
But all I can hear is the bum, bum, bum!

Justin Bieber looks quite fine,
But his voice crosses the high line!

Robbie Williams just wants to rock,
But it's time for him to stop!

Lady GaGa is not a mess,
But look at the dress!

ABBA used to make the mams shake it,
But I'm really sorry, I'd rather sit!

Subo is quite the opera queen,
But she looks old and mean!

Jedward has the nursery factor,
But I just watch in laughter!

It might not seem it, there's a lot I like,
Just go and grab your own mic!

Natalie Blyth (14)
Academy 360, Sunderland

The Sound

Music can be slow,
Smooth or upbeat.
You can listen to it by yourself,
Or out loud in the street.

So many artists,
Many styles to choose,
There's jazz and hip hop,
RnB and blues.

Justin Bieber is my fave,
He has the whole image too,
Just playing his CD
Cheers me up when I'm blue.

Rhythm or beat,
Call it whatever you want.
It's all sound and lyrics,
Not the fancy font.

Slip in your earphones,
Switch on your own place.
You can enjoy any music,
Any style, any pace.

Cathryn Cessford
Academy 360, Sunderland

What Matters To Me

My mum is the best,
Better than the rest.
She keeps away the bad
And takes care of my dad.
I love my mum,
She is my chum.

Evan Benson (13)
Academy 360, Sunderland

7

What Matters To Me

Mustangs are what matter to me,
Galloping as fast as the eye can see.
They're never going to stop and turn around,
Because they must flee at every sound.
They're never going to stop and say hello,
The dark, lead stallion runs, the herd must go,
Galloping fast as the eye can see,
Mustangs are what matter to me!

The new spring foals run after each other,
Their energy baffles the watchful mother.
A mustanger gallops by on his steed,
The herd runs with the dark stallion in the lead.
The most beautiful thing I've ever seen,
Mustangs are what matter to me.

If the race is lost, then I will fall,
I'm kind of sick of full stalls.
Mustangs are meant to be wild and free,
Mustangs are what matter to me.

Dionne Clark-Patterson (11)
Academy 360, Sunderland

Untitled

I stand up there upon the stage,
Watching the crowd jump and gaze.
I sing my song,
I hope I don't get my words wrong.
Once the show is over,
I am off to Dover
To have another great show.
The tour comes to an end,
Now it's time to descend.

Jasmine Boyd (13)
Academy 360, Sunderland

Music Matters

A drum beat, a piano, a guitar rhythm or two,
Music that makes you tap your shoe!
A CD player, computer or even an iPod,
Music that makes your mam call you a sod!
A tune that makes you want to rock,
A rhythm that gives your cat a shock!
Lyrics that make you want to cry,
Words that make you jump, dance or sigh.
Music that helps you pray to God,
A tune that introduces cod.
A treble clef, semi quaver or even a crochet,
A song that uses a drum kit.
African, Spanish, sometimes Latin,
A genre that uses dancers in satin.
Play your music loud and proud,
Jump around in a crowd.
Whatever your taste, whatever your passion,
Music is always the latest fashion.

Amy Blyth (14)
Academy 360, Sunderland

What Matters To Me

Dance is what matters to me,
Spinning and turning to see,
Kicks and jumps all around,
But still not a sound.
Music is all you will hear,
If you are near,
Dance is what matters to me.
Freestyle and diva is all I do
And a bit of hip hop too
Dance is the best,
To the right, to the left.
Dance is what matters to me,
My make-up and hair
Makes me feel like I am floating on air.
Dance gives me a thrill,
It makes me feel brill.
As you can see,
Dance is what matters to me.

Jessica Hackett (11)
Academy 360, Sunderland

Which Is What Matters To Me!

I see my hawk hovering above
Looking for a tasty dove
She swoops and dives
Which makes them fly
Which she can use her pace
To catch the chase
Which is what matters to me.

If she's an ounce overweight
Then you've made the mistake
Of thinking she'll fly
Because she'll probably die
Which is what matters to me.

I love my bird
Because she can always be heard
She sits on the perch so pure
Waiting for me to get out the lure
My kestrel, Cassie, is what matters to me.

Billy Sayers (13)
Academy 360, Sunderland

Halloween

You're out at night
And there's something in flight
That's given you a fright.

Does it ride on a broom?
What's that *boom, boom?*

As I approached the door,
Something dropped to the floor.

As I turned around to see,
There was a witch facing me.

She called for a cat
That appeared on the mat.

They both looked at my face
And said that will do for Grace.

Then they jumped on the broom
And we were off in a zoom.

Beth Bosher (13)
Academy 360, Sunderland

What Matters To Me

Tyler is funny,
Ellie has a bunny,
She named it Honey,
Tiegan has money.

Ruth is cute,
She plays the flute,
Oh, how she's good,
Friends are what matters to me.

Natasha is cool,
I see her in school,
Lauryn is pretty,
And she likes 'Hello Kitty'.

Charlette is tall,
I am small,
I love my friends,
Friends are what matters to me.

Courtney Taylor (11)
Academy 360, Sunderland

What Matters To Me

I love my brother, he's funny
And he loves my two bunnies.
He's only two, he's got the flu
And that's what matters to me.

My little brother loves Scooby-Doo,
He barks like a dog,
He sits on the bog
And that's what matters to me.

My little brother is cuddly
And plays with cars,
He likes to read books
And that's what matters to me.

I love my brother,
I do, I truly do
And that's what matters to me.

Caitlin Edmundson (12)
Academy 360, Sunderland

What Matters To Me?

Horses matter to me,
Cantering by bending the knee.
Leaping over the jump,
And landing with a bit of a bump.

Horses matter to me,
When I pay the stable fee.
I never have much money left in my pocket,
And I have a picture of my horse in a locket.

Horses matter to me,
My horse is a she.
She is a beautiful dapple grey,
And she always gets her own way.

Tiegan Bridge (11)
Academy 360, Sunderland

FIFA II

FIFA II is my life,
When I play it, I'm as sharp as a knife!
No one can beat me,
They tremble when they meet me.
I play Liverpool all day long,
So I can sing the Kop song.
I play Man United for the thrill,
Because I win 4-0!
I won the Barclays Premier League,
I took it by siege.
Then I take on the Champion's Cup,
But all I do is mop up.
Every season I win the treble,
My dad calls me incredible!

Darryl Aldred
Academy 360, Sunderland

To Tell St Peter

On patrol in Afghan, sand blowing at my face,
Not a sound of movement, a total desolate place.
Six men in my squad, my artillery mateys,
Each of them armed with an SA80.

My commanding officer, brought us to a stop,
The sound of a rifle, went off with a pop.
We opened fire, on the men who wanted our lives,
We fought and we fought, for survival we strived.

A flash of white, a jolt of pain,
My earthly body bound in chains.
And when I get to Heaven, to St Peter I will tell,
'One more soldier reporting, sir, I've served my time in Hell.'

Alex McMahon (13)
Academy 360, Sunderland

My Gran

You are the teddy I cuddle up to at night
You are the stars so shiny and bright

You are my tears I always cry
You are the one who never says bye

You are the picture I look at every day
You are the one who says you will always stay

You are the brush that brushes my hair
You are the one who broke my chair

You are the one who takes me out
You are the one who never shouts

You are the one who put my name in a book
You are the one who gives me that look

You are my darkness I see in the sky
You are the one who tells me to try

You are the drift that sends me to sleep
You are the one that loves all the sheep

You are the one that says get away from the bullies
You are the one that always worries

You are the one who said you would come into school
You are the one that jumps in the pool

You are the one who says you will beat them up
You are the one who makes me jump

After that night I go into school
Just about to write a poem all about you

A teacher comes in and says my name
I go out of the room going insane

My cousin picks me and Abby up and takes us to your house
We get out of the car and you're all on the grass

They take us inside and sit us down
We look at each other and we start to frown

They tell us the news and we try to stay strong
But when we look at your chair we think it's too long

Our hearts start to break in two
All we're doing is thinking of you

Right at this moment my heart starts to sink
I open my eyes and everything is pink

I go outside and start to go mad
But one thing I need to say is that . . .

I love you and I miss you,
Gran!

Sophie McCann
Ashton Community Science College, Preston

Media

Music, Facebook and Internet
I love it like I love my pets
It's all the same when all gets wet
It's music, Facebook and Internet

When music becomes the subject
It gets quite physical
When I spit some bars the madness is lyrical
When I drink juice the taste is tropical
Cos it's music, Facebook and Internet

Facebook is great
Facebook is my life
Facebook is just as good as my wife
I wouldn't stab it with a knife
Cos it's music, Facebook and Internet

Internet is amazing
It's great for lazing
It's got loads of megabytes
Not the food but gigabytes
It's got email, games and Google
It's the brain I never had for my homework on moodle.

Samson Ogundaisi (12)
Ashton Community Science College, Preston

My Friends

I have a friend,
I have a friend called Sophie,
I've known her most of my life,
She's the funny one out of us,
Funny and loud,
But she's not my best friend anymore,
Now she's more of a sister.

I have a friend,
I have a friend called Hannah,
I've known her a few months now,
She's the jokey one out of us,
Jokey and funny.
I hope we'll be friends all through high school and more.

I have a friend,
I have a friend called Anna.
I've known her a few months now,
She's the quiet one out of us,
Quiet and friendly.
I can tell we are friends and always will be.

I have a friend,
I have a friend called Rachael.
Again, I've known her a few months now.
She's the loud one out of us,
Loud and funny.
I hope we will be friends all through high school.

I love my friends!

Megan Goulding (12)
Ashton Community Science College, Preston

Money, Music And Football

I wanna be famous
I wanna be a star
I wanna own a bar
And buy nice cars.

Play the music
Loud and clear
You think you're something special
With your looney tunes.
Guitar, drums, keyboards and bass
So loud, I can hear it from space.

Liverpool, PNE, the places I'd like to stay
Scoring goals from 30 yards away.
If I stay, we'll win the crown
People wanna meet me all over the town.
Steven Gerrard, Jamie Carragher
They are legends
In a few years they'll come to mention
Istanbul 2005, 3-0 down at half-time to win on penalties.
Gee, what a place to be.
Preston, Preston, who would've guessed 'em?
4-1 down at Leeds ya see
You can't question their determination when you see the scoreline:
6-4 to the North End.
Oh yes, whatta guess, Parkin hat-trick, he passed the test.
I want his autograph and so do the rest.

Caius McCrone (12)
Ashton Community Science College, Preston

Music Is My Life

My iPod is my life,
It's always in my hand.
I just sit there listenin'
To my favourite band.
Sitting there listenin'
Beats blastin' in my ear,
Lost in my own world,
I like what I hear.
I cry when it's silent,
I laugh when it's loud,
I'm addicted to music,
I don't care, I'm proud.
I'm lost without music,
Without it I'd die,
I'd say I'm OK
But that would be a lie.
Dance is my movement,
I adore the beat,
When the tunes are blastin',
I can't control my feet.
I just can't explain
How music is my life,
It gives me a good feelin'
When beats and rhythms are rife.

Lauren Jeffrey (13)
Ashton Community Science College, Preston

Football

The name of the game is football.
You have to get the ball in the goal.
Tackles and overhead kicks and also tricks.
Fans cheer all the time, like it is a rhyme.

Jordan Bate (12)
Ashton Community Science College, Preston

Music

First we start with something soft
Maybe BOB or Bruno Mars
Then we move it up a step
To 'Written In The Stars'

Then we get some rap
Eminem, Plan B, The Streets
Turn up the speakers
Bringing up the heat

And then we get to the best bit
Dubstep all the way
Turn up the speakers to their highest
Brighten up my day

And then there is a shouting noise
Somewhere in the background
I can only guess who it is
It's my mum making that sound

'Turn that down!' she shouts
'I can hardly hear it myself!' I reply
But I turn it down anyway
I'll have to wait until she's gone
To let the music fly.

Robert Massey (12)
Ashton Community Science College, Preston

Football

Me 'n ma mates are cool
We support the team Liverpool
We go to every game
Our shirts always the same
Liverpool are the best
Better than all the rest.

Jack Herd (13)
Ashton Community Science College, Preston

School

I need my education and lots of dedication
For my graduation.
This is not my imagination.
I intend to fulfil it,
So I shout out to the nation.
Those who go to school will rule
And those who don't will drool.
So don't be a fool, go to school.
I'd rather get a job than be a mugger
To get some money.
I'd never be a thug and drink and use drugs
And live life with a knife,
Because where would that get me?
I'd never steal a car,
I'd never have a fight
Because where would that get me?
In jail and I'd rather be free
Than be under strict law,
Wouldn't you?

Tyreece Franklin (11)
Ashton Community Science College, Preston

Fishing

Fishing is so cool, I always get a bite,
I lift my rod up and it's a little pike.

Sometimes I get a big fish on the end of my rod,
I hope I've got a big enough dish.

I think to myself, what am I going to do?
Should I let it out or should I let it go?
Or should I shout, 'Help! There's a big fish on the end of my rod
And it's not letting go!'

Daniel Evans (11)
Ashton Community Science College, Preston

Life Poem

Life's a bum
So respect your mum.
Learn your education or you'll just stay dumb.
Got four fingers and just one thumb,
Respect them cos what would you do without them?
'Cause listen love, life's hard but get on with it,
It can be good, like rays of sun,
Or bad like the colour of mud.
Life brings opportunities, so take one when you can,
Everyone can do something, it's not all man.
Man-made cars and man-made tables,
Don't think all girls can do is pull off labels.
Life is a game, so play it right, 'cause sometimes it's right to be Mr Nice
Guy,
I got my inspiration off a friend of mine.
We started to rap and the term 'spittin' as a joke
When something came into mind.
This could be real, this could be true,
Lauren Jeffrey's the girl that made my dreams come true.

Corrie Hewitt (12)
Ashton Community Science College, Preston

My Family

My family matters to me the most.
They are always there for me
When I'm sad or happy.
My dog is one of my best mates.
He always cheers me up
When I have an awkward day at school
And then he sits by me all the time.
My nan is always kind like my grandma and grandads.
This is my family and they will never change.

Lewis Danvers (12)
Ashton Community Science College, Preston

Winter

I love winter,
The rain and the cold,
Most importantly, the snow.

Halloween ain't bad at all,
Someone down my street is dressing as Cheryl Cole.
Why not witches, devils, or maybe a zombie,
Or even a skeleton wearing Wellingtons.

Bonfire Night ain't bad at all,
It's not all fireworks,
But who am I kidding?
All the different colours,
Gold, pink, red, blue,
Eeeek! *Baaannnggg!*

Over all of them,
Christmas is the best,
The presents are awesome,
It's about having your family, in my opinion.

Katie Reid (12)
Ashton Community Science College, Preston

My Life!

I like my horses and there are no causes,
I like my friends and the friendship we have,
I like my pets and they matter to me,
I like my family and they mean a lot.

At school I like the teachers because they're friendly,
I'm at school now, well high school,
And I have made lots of new friends.
I know my stuff because I'm cool,
At least I've still got my primary school friends
And I am pleased.

Hannah Bryans (11)
Ashton Community Science College, Preston

Fudge

Creamy fudge is really cool
If you don't eat it
You're a fool!

Crumbly like an Oxo
But not coming
In a boxo!

Vanilla fudge!
Chocolate fudge!
Butter fudge!

People grumble on which to buy
But I just say
Why?

Because . . .

All fudge is really cool
If you don't eat it
You're a fool!

Taylor Donoughue-Smith [11]
Ashton Community Science College, Preston

Scouting

A campfire is a desire
Camping outdoors to explore
Mapping is team roaming

A campfire is a desire
Outdoor exploring
I adore.

Canoeing in the river flowing.

While I'm napping, the tent door flapping
Sizzling sausages frying in my pan
Cooking as fast as they can.

Byron Molyneux [11]
Ashton Community Science College, Preston

Fashion And Friends

F unky, fabulous
A lways there for me
S hows beautiful colours
H appy memories, happy times
I ndependent
O n my own
N ever far away

A lways together
N ever alone
D o everything

F orever
R eally amazing
I will always love them
E very day is magical
N ever alone
D etermination to look after each other
S hows love and affection.

Courtney Mitchell (11)
Ashton Community Science College, Preston

A Family

Families are always there for you,
Through the good times and the rough,
Whenever you need them at all.
You can trust them through the day,
Because they will love you always,
Anytime, any way.
A family is the best
And you love them all to bits,
They make you laugh and make you smile.

A family holds your hands for a moment,
But holds your hearts forever.

Jasmine Maddox (11)
Ashton Community Science College, Preston

I Wanna Be Famous

I wanna be famous,
I wanna be a star,
I want loads of money
And I wanna buy a car.

I want my picture on the back of The Sun,
Scoring goals against everyone,
Liverpool, Chelsea, don't stand a chance,
Then even Barca might give me a glance.

Music is pop, it's rap, hip hop,
Every music deal wants to give me a shot.
Guitar, keyboard, drums and bass,
It's so loud you can hear it from space.

I wanna be famous,
I wanna be a star,
I want loads of money
And I wanna buy a car.

Josh Bate (12)
Ashton Community Science College, Preston

Have You Ever?

Have you ever had a big secret
That you couldn't even tell your best friend?
Have you ever had a big secret
That if it slipped out, your world would end?
Have you ever had a secret
That makes you hurt all day?
Have you ever had a secret
That you would not shout hooray?
Have you ever had a secret
That is as secret as a secret can be?
Well, if you have . . .
I bet you won't tell me!

Charlie Parkhill (12)
Ashton Community Science College, Preston

My Mum

My mum is such a bum
She thinks I love to hum
But the truth is I really don't
Anyway she won't listen to me
Even though it's in my poetry.

I tell her every day and night
And I give her such a fright
Someday I just think she might
Just listen to me
Even though it's in my poetry.

Every time we go somewhere
I try to really annoy her
Because she thinks I love to hum
But I guess that's my mum
Who just won't listen to me
Even though it's in my poetry.

Melissa Newsham (12)
Ashton Community Science College, Preston

Things That Matter

I love my cat
Even though she is fat.
I stroke her as she sleeps on the mat.
I love my mum and dad,
Even though they can get a bit mad,
Then shout at me when I am bad.
I love my nan,
She loves to drive her van,
She loves to sit in front of the fan.

Lois Atkinson (12)
Ashton Community Science College, Preston

Football Frenzies

Every footballer has to win
If not they get the bin
Today is all about the tactics
And the hat-tricks
It's all about the fans
And the plans
Kick-off
The team starts to pass
The ball is rolling on the grass
A player takes a kick
The ball is played through offside
'Oh yes,' shouts the defender with pride
A player is running fast
He is through
He has a blast . . . goal!
It came off the pole!

Aaron Reay (11)
Ashton Community Science College, Preston

Chocolate And Sweets

When I eat a chocolate Twix
A little chocolate mix
In my mind I go very far
When I eat the chocolate bar.

I love chocolate so much
When I give it a little touch
I'll eat it any time
And it's all mine.

I like sweets as well
Just keep it a secret, don't tell
I like sweet and sour
I've just got more girl power.

Megan Pill (11)
Ashton Community Science College, Preston

September

Roses are red,
Violets are blue,
September's here,
But have no fear.
We're going to have so much fun,
When we go out and play in the sun.
There's something in September,
That I know you'll remember.
You start school,
But act like a fool,
They will send you out,
With a big shout.
School may be like a boring giraffe,
But you sure will have a great big laugh.
So make school your friend
And your luck will never end.

Katie Simpson (12)
Ashton Community Science College, Preston

Space

10, 9, 8, 7, 6, 5, 4, 3, 2, 1
Blast-off! Shooting off, shaking all over the place,
All is dark, we're in space.

Look out and this view won't last,
It is the red planet and accidentally hit blast.

Speeding towards it at full speed,
Try to hit land just like a weed.

I crash and I bang and now I'm stuck on Mars,
Please say the Martians have space cars.

Riding the Mars Rover here and there,
Speeding around, but I don't know where.

Chloe Moon (12)
Ashton Community Science College, Preston

Life Ain't Perfect

These are the things I hate the most,
Dying, lying and people that boast.
Bullying, fighting, just say it to my face,
Sometimes love but most of all race.
Child abuse, drugs, why do they make it?
They call me dumb, but they're the ones who take it.
Animal cruelty, 9/11, now they're in a better place,
That's called Heaven.
My grandad survived the Second World War.
It's like they have to do it, it's like their law.
Blackpool scum by the sea,
We all love PNE.
Family fighting, it hurts me a lot,
It hurts that much, it's like I've been shot.
Now you know what I dislike,
Come on Preston, you lily-whites!

Kain Innes (12)
Ashton Community Science College, Preston

Me And My Boyfriend

I have a boyfriend called Samuel
He's funny and kind
And he's always there for me when I need him.
I go to his house every day
And we go to the park for a chat
And he tells me what he has done that day.
Sometimes we go for a little walk
Around the park and street
And I think we will stay together forever and always!

Courtney Mason (11)
Ashton Community Science College, Preston

Which One To Take?

I've been eating my food
But I'm in a mood
Now I need a drink
But I'd better think
Maybe a beer
It would make me cheer
Or maybe a cola
Who knows, I might get taller
Or maybe a tea
But I might need a pee.

Maybe I should get milk
But it might spill over my shirt which is silk
Now I've got to think
Which one to take
Or maybe I should just bake a cake!

Aamir Ali Anjum (12)
Ashton Community Science College, Preston

My Bed

I love my bed, it's nice and warm,
When I'm in it, it makes me yawn.
I wake up at 10am,
Wanting to go back in it again!

I love my bed, it's nice and warm,
When I'm in it, it makes me yawn.
I feel safe under the covers,
I'm not hiding from the dark,
I'm hiding from my horrid brothers.

I love my bed, it's nice and warm,
When I'm in it, it makes me yawn.
I'm off to sleep, so goodbye,
When I wake up I'll say hi!

Katie Herd (13)
Ashton Community Science College, Preston

The Things That Matter To Me

I love my boyfriend,
He's so sweet,
He makes me laugh and gives me treats.

I love my family,
They're so cool,
They like playing in the pool.

I hate people that are moody,
So why don't they just turn doody?
Some are chavs, some think they're cool,
But I just think they're all tools.

I hate death and terrorists,
So I think these shouldn't exist.
It makes me cry to see you die,
But I pray to God to say hi.

Samantha Reynolds (12)
Ashton Community Science College, Preston

Friends

I like my friends, yes I do,
And I've made even more since I came to high school
And still I've kept my old friends since I made my new,
I like them all and they all like me too.

Some I've known since the beginning,
And some I've only just met.
Some I met inbetween
And some I have not found yet.

Alice Young (11)
Ashton Community Science College, Preston

Wagon Wheels To After Eights

Wagon Wheels to beefy meals
From full on steak to After Eights
Hot dog buns to hot cross buns
Chocolate bunnies as sweet as honey

Skinny nuns eating hot dog buns
Funny geeks eating mouldy leeks
A Preston fan eating more than my nan
But wait . . .
Where are my After Eights?

My After Eights, no my uncle's steak
After Eights, no they're her dates
After Eights, no that guy's fishing bait
After Eights, oh my God, is that my best mates
With my empty box of After Eights?

Harry Jolly (13)
Ashton Community Science College, Preston

Friendships

Some friendships are full of laughter and days out
Some friendships are full of memories I can't read out
Some friendships are made to last a lifetime

Friends, you can talk to when you're feeling down
Friends, you can play with when you want to get out
Friends, are there for you all the time.

Friendships are made to keep going until the end
Friendships will have some small breaks
Where arguments are formed
Well, that's what friendship's all about
Arguments will stop if you stop them

It takes a moment to make a friend . . .
But it takes a lifetime to be a friend!

Anna Noblet (11)
Ashton Community Science College, Preston

My Poem About Football

I'm football mad, oh yes I am
I know my stuff so I'm not bad
People think that I am the best
But that's obvious because I'm from the north west.

I'm a Preston fan till I die
I'm football mad
But you probably know that.

I have been to five away games
And we have won every single time
My favourite player is Wayne Rooney
He acts in a movie called Shrek.

I like his wife, I certainly do
I wouldn't mind if she made me a brew.

Adam McLoughlin (11)
Ashton Community Science College, Preston

Liverpool FC

Liverpool FC is the club for me,
I love to watch them on TV,
I would like to go to their ground,
But my dad says it's a lot of pounds.

They've won lots of cups,
Which makes me very proud,
I sing along with
'You'll Never Walk Alone'.

Matthew Wilcock (11)
Ashton Community Science College, Preston

Why Does It Happen?

All these people having fights
Guns and knives and baseball bats
All these objects all take lives
All these people hurt and marked
But all to a better place.
Why does it happen?

Alicia Hindle (12)
Ashton Community Science College, Preston

Liverpool FC

Liverpool, Liverpool, Liverpool FC
Liverpool is the team for me
A great line-up dressed in red
I can't get Liverpool out of my head
Liverpool, Liverpool, Liverpool FC
Liverpool is the team for me

Keep your Chelsea, Everton too
Why support a team in blue?
On our way to Anfield we go
Watch the Reds put on a show
Liverpool, Liverpool, Liverpool FC
Liverpool is the team for me

Fill my heart with cheer and pride
They are the one and only side
Liverpool, Liverpool, Liverpool FC
Liverpool is the team for me.

Callum Robinson (12)
Chesterfield High School, Crosby

My Brother

He may be annoying
He may be mean
He may always want to make a scene

I support Everton
He supports Liverpool
He sometimes can be a complete fool

I like dancing
He likes football
I will always pick him up when he falls

He may do my head in
He may always want to win
But he's my brother and I love him

He sometimes takes it over the line
But I'm so glad
That he's all mine.

Rebecca Lynch (13)
Chesterfield High School, Crosby

Untitled

My favourite thing is sports
And getting to play on netball courts.
When I am warming up,
I feel like I'm training for the World Cup.
I like playing tennis to win a rally,
But love gym performances and the big finale.
When it comes to sport,
I will get marked 'good' on my report,
But when it comes to maths,
I get an F and made to do 100 lengths of the baths.

Natasha McGrath
Chesterfield High School, Crosby

A Place That Matters To Me

Coniston is in the Lake District
We take a caravan there every year
There is loads of sun, including sights to see
This is why Coniston is the place to be.

Climbing mountains to see as far as you can
Going out for tea very happily
To be merry, full of glee
This is why Coniston is the place to be.

Something different every day
Sometimes standing on the pebble beach
Watching the gondola go out on the lake
This is why Coniston is the place to be.

Adam Waggott (13)
Chesterfield High School, Crosby

What Matters To Me . . . Family

F amily are there through the good and bad times
A nd are always there to love you
M ums and dads are always there to pick up pieces when things
    go wrong
I love them and always will
L ove is infinite in all families and relationships
Y ou shouldn't take it for granted.

Leoni Bradshaw
Chesterfield High School, Crosby

Home

I live in a bin
Far, far away
I spend my time
There every day

It is cosy and warm
It has its own wheels
I hunt rats
For my evening meals!

I ride around
Now wheeling away
Sometimes on the motorway

I travel the world
In my very own bin
I think this is
An epic win.

But then one day
The bin fell over
And then it got hit
By a huge bulldozer!

It flew so high
Burning in the sky
I start to cry
I'm going to die

My bin is dead
I don't have a bed
Oh, I will miss my bin.

Liam Taylor (14)
Hesketh Fletcher High School, Atherton

Home

Home, the place I should love to be.
The place where people should love, cherish, care about me.
The place where I should chill with friends and family.
The place where I should have food or drink whenever I need.

But no, it's not like that, no, not here.
When I come home, I'm trembling with fear.
Wondering why? When? How?
It could happen in a few hours, few minutes, maybe even now.

Are they hiding round the corner? Or maybe they've nipped out,
They often are nipping out, round and about.

I go to my room, even though it's so empty and bare.
A bed with a sheet here, a box with a few clothes there.
That's all there is to it, I hate it so much.
So dull, boring, no colour, not a touch.

A few hours later, I hear a door slam, then someone calls my name.
Slowly, I plod downstairs, waiting to feel the pain.

'Hurry up!' they scream and shout.
'After this, we're going back out.'
I walk over to them and then stop and stare.
I think to myself, hold on, these people are my parents,
Surely they must care.

Tonight, something's different, something doesn't seem right.
Okay, I know what they do isn't right anyway,
But it seems different to any other night.
There's a gleam in their eyes and a weird smile on their face.
But strangely, nothing different happens, same strength, same routines, and
same pace.

Fifteen minutes of them beating me, no reason for it at all.
So much for Mum and Dad, I should use their real names, Sarah and Paul.

I can't take it any longer, 11 years is it.
I need it all to stop, I can't take another hit.
I'm sick of it, I need someone to tell.
But who? My neighbour Tracy? My best friend, Tanya?
I know, my favourite teacher, Miss Bell!

But I feel so ashamed and what if they think I'm lying?
But I suppose it's a try, and it's better than always crying.

The next day I go to school and rush to find Miss Bell.
I tell her I need her in private, then I start to tell.

When I finish, she doesn't tell me to stop lying or stop making up stuff.
I can tell by her face, she knows it isn't a bluff.

She looks so stunned, so close to tears.
She says, 'Why didn't you tell me through all these years?'
I tell her I'm scared and she asks scared of what?
Getting more bruises, I say. She asks how many I've got.

I show her them all and she says, 'Right, come on,
We're going to the police to see PC John.
He deals with things like this.'
'Have I done anything wrong, Miss?'

'No, no, no, you've done nothing wrong at all.
Now follow me, I'm just making a call.'

I follow her, she grabs her phone and we go to the car.
We drive to the police station which isn't that far.
They tell me it's all over, nothing more will be done.
They tell me to go over to the kids' area, to go and have some fun.

How can I have fun? I think, but I nod my head and go to the kids' park.
I sit on the swing and look around, I see children play, mums gossip, dogs bark.

I feel so lonely and somehow envious, watching the children with their perfect mum and dad.
It only makes me angrier, at the mum and dad I had.

Leoni Ramsbottom (13)
Hesketh Fletcher High School, Atherton

Home

'Is the place where one lives, belongs or was born'
Is the dictionary definition but people question
As the TV stud on makeover shows says
'It's purely an accessory'
But I tend to disagree
A home is not made from bricks and mortar
Nor builders and men
A home does not need to have walls or a roof over your head
A home is where you feel most happy, most loved

But there is an epidemic sweeping through our great nation
Of kids in care and no one there to wipe away their tears
'Cause when they scream at night, everyone turns a deaf ear
Of mums and dads getting mad and abuse being a common factor
These children have no such thing as 'home'
And souls are searching for peace
But with the power of poetry I hope to raise the subject people fear
A conversation stopper
A thing to make you shudder
An elephant not just in the room but in society

This is the message the world should know
The kids out there are the new generation
But without a home
The future is looking black
We can save these children and start fighting back
Because after all, what we all need and treasure
Is our home.

Abigail Walker (13)
Hesketh Fletcher High School, Atherton

My Lovely Home

My home, my lovely home,
The place I live,
To live my life,
My home is the best.

My home, my lovely home,
Where I get taken care of,
Food, drinks and many more,
My lovely home.

My home, my lovely home,
Where I'm comforted and warm
And always feel safe.

My home, my lovely family home,
My family love me,
My mum, dad and bro.

I may say,
I hate them sometimes,
But when I think,
They are the ones who love
And care for me.

My home is full of laughter,
The place you want to be,
But it's mine to live in always,
My home, my lovely home.

Chelsea Calland (12)
Hesketh Fletcher High School, Atherton

My Friends

My friends are the best
They treat me as a special guest
The fun and the laughter
Always friends forever after.

Sometimes we fall out
What good is that about?
We are all back friends
No more fallout, it all depends.

Four of us walking home
A random talk of the Millennium Dome
We all laugh at the one who's daft
Talking like it is witchcraft.

Connor comes round on the trampoline
I bounce so high I can't be seen
We both have a laugh with my little brother
He takes it too far and tells the mother.

The best friends I have ever had
Friends forever, I'll never forget
If they were criminals I would regret
But they're the best friends I've ever met.

Callum Fairhurst (13)
Hesketh Fletcher High School, Atherton

Home

The warmest welcome, I sense,
All my memories are buried at the heart,
No one knows how I feel,
A family around me, for which I care and love.

Even when I'm all alone,
There's still someone with me,
Drowning my presence with comfort . . .

My door opens, the room buzzes with delight,
My family and friends pour in,
And the vivacity of the mood
Fills me with tears.

As the years drag by,
And the days get shorter,
I think . . .
About the good times, the bad times, the exciting times,
The reality kicks in and I smile.

Now I am old,
I can't cope by myself,
Thinking now, there's no such thing as a perfect home,
But the memories that I have will never fade.

Sophie Turner (13)
Hesketh Fletcher High School, Atherton

Bedroom

Bedroom, bedroom, I wonder where,
How do I put it, it's quite rare!
Mum and Dad are quite fair,
My room I call my lair.

Outside inside, inside out,
These are the things I think about,
Today, tomorrow, never sorrow
And sometimes I feel the need to borrow.

After I walk to my dorm,
In a way, one special form,
Go in, have a look, maybe even read a book,
Up and down, I fall to sleep,
Never ever feel to weep.

My bedroom's my home,
Where I love my white dove,
Thinking, thinking, in a gaze,
This, my only place,
Just one single, never-ending maze.

Bedroom, bedroom, I wonder why,
This is where I sleep tonight.

Keegan Nolan (13)
Hesketh Fletcher High School, Atherton

Home Is A House!

I love to go
I love to go

There's a place in my home,
I love to go,
It's peaceful and calm,
And a bit smelly.

I love to go
I love to go

I go, I go,
I go there all the time,
That's where I go,
I go to rhyme.

I love to go
I love to go

I go there to do my make-up,
I go, I go,
I go to play my games.

I love to go,
It is my bedroom.

Samantha Fildes (12)
Hesketh Fletcher High School, Atherton

The Big Performance

It made us passionate,
As well as unfaithful.

The fast pumping blood
Of the very first kiss,
With a brush on the
Soft, sweet lips.

The happiest moments
In our unique lives,
To the agonising wait,
Knowing it will end.

These are all parts
Of my big performance,
An act of life.

'Planet Earth' is my stage,
I am proud to say
At the end of my performance,
'I have executed it.'

Although another story begins . . .

Connor Warren Calland (13)
Hesketh Fletcher High School, Atherton

Bullies

I was sitting there twiddling my thumbs,
The bullies ran over and bruised my gums.

I went to the teacher,
But he didn't believe me,
I'm hurt right now,
Can't anyone see?

I knew this was going to happen,
I wish it wasn't me,
I know I should have stuck to grime,
It was just us three.

I'm trying to make friends,
But no one likes me,
My life's going to end,
On the count of three . . .

Katie Roberts (13)
Hesketh Fletcher High School, Atherton

My Rooms

My kitchen, my kitchen,
The kitchen is the place I go.
Walked downstairs going from high to low,
Reached the kitchen and banged my toe.

My living room, my living room,
The living room, wonderful luxury,
Big TV, surround sound,
Hands down couch, finding all those pounds.

My bedroom, my bedroom,
Cosy, snuggly and dreamy.
When it's time for bed,
It's that cosy, I'm so still I could be dead.

Jade Griffiths (12)
Hesketh Fletcher High School, Atherton

My Home

My home is a place
Like no other.
We sit and watch
But we love each other.
Me, my brother,
Mum and Dad,
I don't want anything
Better than I've ever had.
I love my family
And they love me,
That's how it'll stay
Forever with me.

Rebecca Colton (13)
Hesketh Fletcher High School, Atherton

My Life

My passion for music is eternal,
My love for the old stuff is great,
I hate all the new stuff at the moment,
But we will just have to wait.

Family and friends are my world,
They look after me every day,
Some may get on my nerves,
But I'd be nothing if they went away.

Skateboarding is my hobby,
That's just me,
Riding, grinding,
And always will be.

Good grades is all I ask for,
They will help me through life,
Get a good job, start a family,
And have a beautiful wife.

Nathan Peloe (13)
Litherland High School, Liverpool

My Life!

Life
Is like Marmite
You either love it
Or hate it.
Memories
Are like a train
They come
And go.
Family and friends
Are precious
But when they're gone
It's not the same.
Photos
Are like a story
They tell the good times
And the bad.
My work
Shows who I am
What I'm capable of
And what I don't get.
My belongings
Are mine
Precious
And safe.
Life
Is like Marmite
You either love it
Or hate it.

Amy McCarthy (12)
Litherland High School, Liverpool

As Life Goes On . . .

Life . . .
Is like a football match,
Where you do make mistakes,
Family and friends . . .
Each like a diamond,
The light in my day.
The quillo . . .
This my auntie made,
It's a quilt and pillow in one,
It's there when I'm lonely.
Photos . . .
They're what I took,
And will be the memories but,
Don't worry they're safe with me.
Laptop . . .
This is the thing I'm addicted to,
I save my memories like photos,
Messages
For when I go back to take a peek.
Memories . . .
They are my life,
I can always remember,
The days when I was young,
And the days as I got older.
My phone . . .
It's there when I need to be safe,
To get in touch with my relatives,
If I ever need help,
My phone is there for me.
Art things . . .
I like to make things,
Rather than buy,
They're memories that I admire
I'd keep them till I die.
Education at school . . .
It's my whole life's work,
I want a good career and . . .
Make my life keep on going.

Responsibility . . .
I'm the one that's responsible,
For the things that I may do,
The little or big things,
It's my choice of what I should do.
People I've lost . . .
They're much safer up there,
Than they would be down here,
When I think of them,
I cry a single tear,
I look up to see the stars,
And I say to myself, there's you.
House fire . . .
I had a house fire,
And lost all the things I admire,
I wasn't that worried,
But all the things that have gone,
It feels like they have been buried,
As we say . . .
Life . . .
Is like a football match,
Where you do make mistakes.

Katie-Jo McGuinness (13)
Litherland High School, Liverpool

Destiny

Life is like a book
Destiny is not written for us but by us
Love and life combine together
To make everyone want
To live forever.

As chapter by chapter
Our life goes by
Love makes people
Laugh and cry.

Jack Maher (12)
Litherland High School, Liverpool

My Poem

I listen to my family
I drink and eat with my family
I'm there with my family
But what am I without them?

I have my house for a reason
For a sleep
A drink
A bite to eat
A nice sweet or a treat
But what am I without it?

I laugh with my friends
It feels like they care
From every bone to every hair
But they're there
But what am I without them?

I need clothes to keep me clean
Healthy and hygienic
From baby clothes, toddler and teen
My soft clothes with the silk
But what am I without them?

A good education will get me through life
Not ruining it with a sharp knife
But it's there for me to do
One chance, but not two
But what am I if I can't do it?

I believe and trust me
I will go on, not give in
I will work as far as the eye can see
I will go on, I will win
But what am I without it?

I think in my head
But when I'm angry it goes red
I will lie down in my bed
My thoughts are there, but won't be said
But what am I without them?

My life is most important of all
I've got my family and friends
Without anything I will fall
My life finishes and ends
But what am I without it?
Nothing!

Joel Redfern (13)
Litherland High School, Liverpool

Bad Day

I wake up
In a bad mood.
People better stay
Out of my way.

People start
Telling me things
'I already know.'
Sooner or later this anger will show.

Coming home from school,
Things are getting better.
I put some music on,
Before my mind is gone.

Anger turns to silence,
Silence.
In my head,
As though everything is dead.

In my dream
I wake up.
My new life
Next to my wife.

I wake up
And realise,
She could be my wife,
So now I'll cling to life.

Danny Bishop (14)
Litherland High School, Liverpool

Things That Matter To Me

Friends
True friends
There's nothing like them
Friends are there for you through highs and lows.

Family
My family loves me
They love me and I love them
I'll love them no matter what
They mean the world to me.

My straighteners
My straighteners make my hair look nice
If they broke
I would cry.

School always bores me
It's my friends that make it fun
English and maths I quite enjoy
I hate history
It's a thing of the past.

My future is a blur
But I will make it clear

My cornet and flute
Make a noise of many
Sometimes they annoy my parents
But I don't care
Music is what I love
And music what I play.

My phone is on contract
I take it everywhere
It's like a second limb to me
When it dies I cry.

On my laptop
I'm on Facebook
Every second of
Every minute of
Every hour of
Every day of
Every week of
Every month of
Every year.

Sally Strom (13)
Litherland High School, Liverpool

They Don't Care . . .

I watch them pass day by day,
They look at me and don't know what to say.
When they see me they give me a look,
They feel top and I'm just muck.
But they don't care . . .

I stick out my hand in hope for money,
They just look at me and think I'm funny.
I sometimes sleep in a damp, dark alley,
I think I'm somewhere by Wood Vale rally.
But they don't care . . .

I didn't choose to be like this, I had no choice,
I wanted to speak out but couldn't find my voice.
I lost my job and my family,
At this point you don't want to be me.
But they don't care . . .

I'd rob a shop, I'd trash a home,
I sold a small glass dome.
I wouldn't kill someone, I wouldn't dare,
I've said it three times, I'll say it again.
But they don't care . . .

Chelsea Mack (13)
Litherland High School, Liverpool

What Matters To Me?

My family matters,
The most to me,
They're loving and caring,
And the best easily.

My friends are funny,
They make me happy,
They matter to me,
Including my PS3.

I love playing golf,
It's so much fun,
It's better than getting moaned at,
By my mum.

My pet dog and tortoise,
Also matter to me,
But sadly they can't give me,
A good GCSE.

Getting good GCSEs,
To get a good career,
So I have lots of money,
To spend throughout the year.

These are the things
That matter most to me,
I'll never take them for granted.

John Grindle (13)
Litherland High School, Liverpool

Things That Matter To Me

Mum's like a best friend
Always there for you
To talk, to cuddle
Or even just to be there.

Brothers are like enemies
Until you get hurt
Or someone hurts you
Then they're like a bodyguard
There to protect you.

Dad's like a cash machine
There to give you money
But when something goes wrong
They are there like mums and brothers.

Family is important to us
Just like friends and lovers
But family is different
We only get one.

So, take nothing for granted
Live life while you can
And be good to your family
While you've got the chance.

Shannon McFadden (13)
Litherland High School, Liverpool

The Passion Poem

Passion is like a flower.
It blooms in the summer sun.
When it blooms your heart fills with happiness,
Warmth and joy.
When it blooms it feels like everything in the world
Just falls into place.

Aimee Porter (13)
Litherland High School, Liverpool

59

Life Poem

Life is about getting along,
Jumping and bumping together.

You need to sit down to have a break,
You sit there in peace having a cake.

My friends are great, we go out together to have a picnic,
We sit there on the grass to watch the butterflies fly.

We all like to be someone famous,
Waiting there with our diamond necklaces.

All over that means that we care about each other,
Me and my best mates have a lot of memories together.

The laughing times, sad times and amazing times,
We all want a good job like anything you ever wanted before.

What matters to me the most is my family,
We love each other so very much . . .

But, you know that . . .
Life is about getting along,
Jumping and bumping together.

Stacey Jones (12)
Litherland High School, Liverpool

What Matters

Trust
Is like a mirror
It can shatter
The pieces can be put back together
There will always be
A crack in your reflection

Memories, some good, some bad
But the ones we mostly treasure
Are in our hearts forever.

Sophie Brown (13)
Litherland High School, Liverpool

What Matters To Me?

My friends and family all matter to me,
Even my pet dog and my Xbox 360.
Going on warm holidays and sunbathing by the sea,
Watching the football and a good GCSE.

My mum and my dad always look after me,
They feed me, they love me as much as can be.
Being an actor matters to me,
Crying and laughing and lots of money!

GCSEs - maths and PE,
Trying to be the best I can be.
My pet dog, Ebony, is big and furry,
I feed her by hand, well ever so nearly.

My friends at school are funny,
They always make me laugh.
They're like a bunch of clowns who are extremely daft.

These are the things that matter to me,
They're all good,
Well, good enough for me.

Derek Millington (13)
Litherland High School, Liverpool

Football

Football is my passion
Football is in my heart
My position is unique
It has stolen my heart
It gives you pain
It gives you gain
I will love it for life
It can be like a piercing knife
It will strike you, help you.

Marc Robinson (13)
Litherland High School, Liverpool

My Family

They say home is
Where the heart is
But that doesn't matter to me.
What matters to me is my family
And all those that are around me.

You have the rough times
The tough times and
Often the good times
But that's what families are made of.

The good, the bad,
The ugly times
But I'm no Clint Eastwood
And sometimes
Christmas feels
Like the Wild West.

But in the end we
All pull together as one big
Family!

Daniel Rowan (13)
Litherland High School, Liverpool

A Dream

A dream is not what you hold in your hand,
But a thing of wonder you keep in your mind.
A dream is like a bubble of love and care,
And just a spoonful of sweetness with a head full of hair.
When you move your hollow head,
Does your dream bubble crash?
When your dreams fall to the floor,
Do you clean it with a mop . . .
Your definition may be different than mine.
Whatever it is, it's a dream.

Vicki Westwell (13)
Litherland High School, Liverpool

My Grandad

When I was born you held me tight.
You told me you were my grandad,
And everything would be alright.
Every day I would sit in your chair.
When you came in you would give me your stare.
You watched me grow until I was nine.
You always called me your 'Little Sunshine'
I would always wear your flat cap.
Help you make the fire.
I watched you do many things that would always inspire.
You're no longer here for me to wear your cap,
Sit on your chair, or on your lap.
But each day, Grandad, doesn't go by without me thinking, asking why?
Now I am older I understand,
I just want to hold your hand.
I look into the sky at night
See a star shining bright.
I know for a fact that star is you.
I love you always, my whole life through.

Kate Carey (12)
Litherland High School, Liverpool

Snoopy

You are black,
And you are white,
You keep me warm every night,
I keep you tight,
Through the night,
In the morning,
I let you go,
You're like a fluffy slipper,
I tighten you up,
You're like a baby caterpillar.

Georgia Harrison (13)
Litherland High School, Liverpool

My Special Family

A family completes the heart,
They love you from the very start.
With a family many feelings occur,
Through happy and sad times
Feelings you share.
Families annoy you and can make you stressed,
But you love them really, they help when you're depressed.
They can make me angry but I'll never hate.
Love and appreciate them now cos
Soon they'll go to Heaven's gate.
The memories we have are amazing and funny.
I remember when I lost my teeth, my brother called me gummy.
When I was three they took me to the zoo.
My dad said the gorilla looked like my nan,
Now I'm twelve, I am obsessed with make-up and fake tan.
Now I've thought I'm really lucky to have one.
But it's different for some people as theirs has already gone.
You will not know how to be,
Without your loving family.

Kirsty Burke (12)
Litherland High School, Liverpool

Baby Cousin

Baby cousin,
Royal and sweet
Kisses and hugs whenever you meet.

Loving and caring,
Always loves sharing
With family and friends.

Baby cousin, oh so sweet
Having her around
Is such a treat.

Erykah Vosilius (12)
Litherland High School, Liverpool

The Hospital

The hospital is where I lay,
Just time to sleep,
No time to play,
Doctors and nurses,
All sorts of curses,
The doctor comes over, I felt some pain,
I fell asleep with the drug, in less pain,
The hospital is where I lay,
Just time to sleep,
No time to play.

Family all around the bed,
Making sure you're not dead,
They all care,
Even though they scare,
You look at them wondering what do they want,
The hospital is where I lay,
Just time to sleep,
No time to play.

Hannah Snelling (13)
Litherland High School, Liverpool

Football

Football, it's a beautiful game.
Played by many. There's plenty of fame.
To see players put others to shame.
The players get all the glory, all the fame.
Football, it's a man's game.
Liverpool, it was a successful team.
The type of club that fulfilled your dreams.
Now the team is falling apart.
Championship football for a new start.

Marc Benson (13)
Litherland High School, Liverpool

Close To My Heart

I have many things,
Close to my heart.
So many things,
Where do I start.

First there is Misty,
My special dog.
I miss her,
So I keep her close to my heart.

Next is Princess,
My best friend.
I see her every day,
So she is close to my heart.

Last but not least,
My family of nine,
Mum, Dad, sisters, brothers
No matter where they are,
They're close to my heart.

Georgia Buchanan (12)
Litherland High School, Liverpool

Untitled

One sunny day, I did something horrible.
Something brutal, nasty, deplorable.
Something for me was truly historical,
But my mother still thought I was cute and adorable.
Am I a murderer? I ended a life.
Although I didn't use a weapon like a gun or a knife.
It was my shoe, an accident of course,
But now I feel great remorse.
I wish I could save it, bring it back.
I can't, I hope it went to Heaven,
It was only an ant.

Shane Glean (13)
Litherland High School, Liverpool

66

I Do Exist You Know

Yes, I'm homeless but I'm no different to you am I?
Apart from having no house that is.
I've walked past you loads of times - probably
My hair is long and scruffy, but that's because I can't afford the old barbers.
And yes, my beard is long, well that keeps my face warm
And I can't afford that either.

When I ask for change, it's because I need it
I wouldn't ask if I didn't, I'm cold and hungry.
Some of you are kind;
Others just laugh and leave me behind.

My blanket is now thin and manky
But I can't afford a new one.
You should be grateful you're not living like me,
No family, no friends, just me, a lonely, cold folk.

Any change please, I'll give you a smile,
I haven't given anyone one of them for a while,
I'm saving it for you.

Chelsea Jones (13)
Litherland High School, Liverpool

What Matters To Me?

Friendship is like a chestnut tree,
Standing there in all its glory.
Trust is like LEGO,
Build it up and up and up.
Friendship is like the sea,
Goes in but can go out.
Trust is like Jenga,
With every piece taken out . . .
It gets weaker.

Mark Percy (12)
Litherland High School, Liverpool

My Precious Things

Many things mean a lot to me,
Most things I can touch,
My house, my teddy and my bracelet,
My laptop, my phone and my iPod,
Some things that mean a lot to me,
Some precious things,
Friendship, safety, love and trust,
I cannot touch,
Bur further still there are some things,
My family, friends and loving animals,
I may be able to touch them,
Yet the relationship you cannot replace,
In this poem,
The most important thing,
Is my family,
They may not be there forever,
Yet in my heart,
They will be.

Sophie Rimmer (12)
Litherland High School, Liverpool

My Family To Me

My family is like a tree
We move from branch to branch
Our friendship is strong
It is to be that for forever long
They have supported me, raised me
Done the best they can
I will love them
And respect them
And do the best I can.

Ethan Pawsey (13)
Litherland High School, Liverpool

Ghosts

They are alone,
They are ignored,
They are poor.
They are like a ghost.

The lonely ghost,
They live in poor conditions.
They look miserable,
And they just wait.

The poor little ghost,
He just wants some toast,
They stand out
They have nowt.

They are different to me and you,
Just look at those pair of ghosts,
Day after day after day,
The ghost there - the poor, unfortunate, homeless person.

Josh Wright (13)
Litherland High School, Liverpool

My Grandad

You've always had a special place deep within my heart.
Forever there it will remain, whether we're near or far apart.
You've always been a favourite to everyone you know.
You've always made me happy when I was feeling low.
The special times we spent together will never be replaced.
Nothing else could ever compare to when I saw a smile upon your face.
Although you got older your name was never mentioned.
You liked to think you were twenty-one when you were near your pension.
I never needed to worry when my mum wasn't there.
Because I always had my grandad, for he had time to spare.
I will always love my grandad, no matter how tall I grow.
For he was my grandad, and that I'll always know.

Liam Price (13)
Litherland High School, Liverpool

Tears Of Anfield

Week in, week out we saw
A disastrous start to the season.
Horrific, horrible, we chanted bye-bye Roy.
Our passion for the game was falling.

Our hate for owners was as bad
As our hate for Man United.
'Yes!' we shouted. 'New owners.'
'Ole, ole, ole, ole!' we chanted. 'We are staying up!'
More and more started to believe
In Roy Hodgson, except for me.
In my mind I was the solution, the cure, the future.

Anfield was electric, the Kop was fabulous,
In Istanbul we won it five times.
Week in, week out we saw a disastrous start to the season.
Horrific, horrible, we chanted bye-bye Roy.
Our passion for the game was falling.

Jack Rimmer (13)
Litherland High School, Liverpool

Enzo

He sits there
All day long
Waiting for me to get home
Howling in the garden
Then, eventually
I'm there.

I play with him all night
Wagging his tail in glee
Then dark falls
Time for bed
The cycle starts
Again!

Ryan Jones (13)
Litherland High School, Liverpool

My Dad Says . . .

My dad says I'm bananas,
But I'm sure I'm an apple.

My dad says I'm nuts,
But I'm sure I'm crisp.

My dad says I'm crackers,
But I'm sure I'm cheese.

My dad says I've lost my marbles,
But I'm sure I never had any marbles.

My dad says I've lost it,
I say lost what?

My dad says I'm insane,
I say no, I'm in the living room.

When I tell my dad he's losing his mind,
He says he hasn't got one to lose.

Helen Duke (13)
Litherland High School, Liverpool

My World

I love my family, friends, boyfriend and my dog.
They are my everything.
My world.
Without them I have nothing.

I idolise Justin Bieber and Cheryl Cole.
They are amazing.
I want to be just like Cheryl.
They are my gods.

But eventually all these will pass away.
When this happens I won't be able to live another day.
Oh how I hope this doesn't come soon.
Or I will be lost without them.

Shannon Lawrenson (13)
Litherland High School, Liverpool

Took For Granted

Pets
Are like friends
Some can be aggressive
Some you could trust with your life
Some show you affection
And others loyalty.

Time is like a rhyme
It flows and goes
It passes through the past and now
It takes out the hate and brings your fate
It helps you mend as if a friend
Time is mine and everyone's to keep
As if it was just a song
Passing through far and long
I wish it was just a bird
Helping time to be heard.

Mathew Morris (13)
Litherland High School, Liverpool

Special Things

My family mean the world to me
They really, really do
I don't know what I'd do without them
I love them lots it's true.

My friends are also special
They are always there for me
I love them so much
Like people love their cups of tea.

Love is all you need
Some people might say
When people break your heart
You're better off that way . . .

Erin Robertson (12)
Litherland High School, Liverpool

Love Is A Feeling

Love is a word that you feel
But never really touch
Something you see
But never really look
Always in heart never in mind
Something that is real
Never fake
You may have regrets
Maybe a mistake
Just remember your loved ones
My friends and family
And that special one
All have a special place in my heart
Maybe miles away
But never really apart
I love them forever!

Rebecca Langton (12)
Litherland High School, Liverpool

Spare Some Change

At home, watching Newsround,
Why don't you give two pounds?
Turn over.

In a café, reading the star,
Send an orphan a Mars bar.
Next page.

At home, knock at the door,
Help me suffer no more,
My dad's not in.

Had a call,
To stop cutting down the tall,
Why doesn't anyone spare some change?

Liam McAdam (13)
Litherland High School, Liverpool

Family

I love my family,
You could never change the way I feel.
I really trust my family,
My emotions swirl like a wheel.
In my family tree,
Love is a big thing,
Although sometimes I get lonely,
I always think of memories.
Sometimes I get upset,
I love the way Mum hugs me.
Although she never frets,
I am always where I should be!
Sometimes Dad's not there,
And yes, I miss him,
But I always think,
He's not that far away.

Lauren Peel (12)
Litherland High School, Liverpool

Love Your Family

They say you can't choose your family
But you can choose your friends,
So what I do is always cherish my family
Deep down in my heart
No matter who they are.
You only get one family
So don't be picky and love your family.
No family is perfect
Not even mine,
But your family
Will always be loving you -
Even if they don't show it to you
They keep it at the back of their heart.

James Good (13)
Litherland High School, Liverpool

Things That Matter To Me

Family
You can love or you can hate
You can laugh or you can cry
You can smile or you can stay shy
No matter what you do
They will be there
For you

But just remember

Brothers
You can hate but also love
They can make you cry
They can make you laugh
Just remember they are your brothers
Love them until
You die!

Chloe Cockburn (12)
Litherland High School, Liverpool

The Love Poem

Love
It is a tingling feeling you get in your heart
When you feel like your legs are jelly
When you feel like he's got a place in your heart
Love isn't easy
Actually
It's more hard
But you can always find a way to make it work
As you can never be apart
Love is something
You won't regret
Love is something
You will not want to forget!

Hannah Callear (12)
Litherland High School, Liverpool

The Joyous Days Of '66

44 years ago this year we all had reason to smile and cheer.
On that day the final score was West Germany 2 - England 4.
But since then nothing's coming our way,
We're still waiting for that fateful day.

Even though we may be down and out,
We still continue to scream and shout,
But we're always kind of loud,
And we're a nation standing proud.

We even continue dreaming with Jules Rimmet still gleaming.
Well those joyous days of '66 in the back of our minds it still sits.
When that fateful day comes once more,
Then the 3 lions shall roar.

44 years ago this year we all had reason to smile and cheer.
On that day the final score was West Germany 2 - England 4.

Ryan Everett (13)
Litherland High School, Liverpool

I Remember

I once had a friend,
I was with him until the very end.

I remember his shining eyes,
That's a memory that never dies.

I remember him in the summer green grass,
Chasing after a ball, he was so fast.

I remember his long white hair,
That was looked after with love and care.

I remember how he loved his food,
If he didn't get it, he would go into a mood.

Only ten years he ever lived for,
I really wish there could have been more.

Mark Sarsero (12)
Litherland High School, Liverpool

Silly Fool

Yo yo yo you silly fool,
Go back to Blackpool,
I'm going to rob your nan,
In my sexy pink transit van,
This rap ain't crap,
So I don't deserve a slap,
Gi's a high five,
And we'll eat cheese and chive,
Crime today should go away,
It shouldn't stay,
Tesco is a shop,
It doesn't sell lots of pop,
Kids have hugs,
But will soon turn to drugs,
Kids should just bail away.

William Bousfield (13)
Litherland High School, Liverpool

Dreams Of A Future Midwife

I'm here to help,
With the baby and the family,
I'm your midwife, Lauren,
So give me a call.

I help deliver your baby,
I give you your belly scan,
I'll check that your baby's looking well.

The first sight of the baby,
The weighing on the scales,
Feeding the first bottle,
Tiny hands and tiny clothes,
Soft skin and button nose.

The pleasure of being a midwife.

Lauren Culshaw (13)
Litherland High School, Liverpool

My Life Of Wonderful Things

I love
My make-up and straighteners
But not like my brothers and sister.
I love watching programmes on TV
But not like my cat, dog and bunny.
I love my clothes, perfume and my big black bag,
But not like my mum and dad.
If I should lose my possessions
I would not shed a tear but
If I lost my family
I would cry for over a year.
It's very nice to have your things but
The best thing in life
Is not what money brings.

Alisha Carton [13]
Litherland High School, Liverpool

Homeless

Broken homes, violence, troubled lives,
Wandering around, lost and alone,
No place to go, no one to see,
On the dirty old never-ending streets.

Starving, lonely, insanity,
Busking, asking, begging,
Living and surviving off other people,
On the dirty old never-ending streets.

Friendless, isolated, lonely,
Never in anyone's mind,
Never given a second thought,
Have you ever thought about us?
Do you care?

Lauren Jones [13]
Litherland High School, Liverpool

Love Is All You Need

It's hard to describe love
But we still know how it feels.
It's not the love you feel for make-up
Or your favourite pair of heels.
The love you feel
For your mum and dad
Is the love you cannot buy.
Like if you lost your phone and make-up
You wouldn't start to cry.
So you love your family
You love your friends
And that's the kind of love
That never ends.

Kelsey Reynolds (13)
Litherland High School, Liverpool

My Football Team

My mum says I'm very healthy,
That could be because I'm very stealthy.

My passion for football is very unique
People say I'll be better if I didn't stand oblique.

I play for a football team
Our trophies always gleam.

There are twins in my team too.
They will always look out for you.

They're not too good,
We will improve,
Otherwise I'm going to move.

David Holt (12)
Litherland High School, Liverpool

Home

When I'm in my home
It is very boring
When I'm playing out
It is very fun
But when I get in a lot of trouble
I wish I was at home

When I'm with my parents
They make me feel embarrassed
When I'm with my friends
They make me feel happy
But when something goes wrong
I wish I was with my parents.

Graham King (13)
Litherland High School, Liverpool

Friends Are The Family We Choose

Friends are the family we choose for ourselves,
The people we love, live and laugh with,
The people we can depend on,
Friends are the family we choose for ourselves,
The people we care for,
The people we are always there for.

Friends are the family we choose for ourselves,
The people we go to,
The people we couldn't live without,
Friends are the family we choose for ourselves,
The people who'll stay with us forever,
They are the family we choose for ourselves.

Megan Miller (14)
Litherland High School, Liverpool

Featured Poets:
DEAD POETS
AKA Mark Grist & MC Mixy

Mark Grist and MC Mixy joined forces to become the 'Dead Poets' in 2008.

Since then Mark and Mixy have been challenging the preconceptions of poetry and hip hop across the country. As 'Dead Poets', they have performed in venues ranging from nightclubs to secondary schools; from festivals to formal dinners. They've appeared on Radio 6 Live with Steve Merchant, they've been on a national tour with Phrased and Confused and debuted their show at the 2010 Edinburgh Fringe, which was a huge success.

Both Mark and Mixy work on solo projects as well as working together as the 'Dead Poets'. Both have been Peterborough's Poet Laureate, with Mixy holding the title for 2010.

The 'Dead Poets' are available for workshops in your school as well as other events. Visit www.deadpoetry.co.uk for further information and to contact the guys!

Read on to pick up some fab writing tips!

Your
WORKSHOPS

In these Workshops we are going to look at writing styles and examine some literary techniques that the 'Dead Poets' use. Grab a pen, and let's go!

Rhythm Workshop

Rhythm in writing is like the beat in music. Rhythm is when certain words are produced more forcefully than others, and may be held for longer duration. The repetition of a pattern is what produces a 'rhythmic effect'. The word rhythm comes from the Greek meaning of 'measured motion'.

Count the number of syllables in your name. Then count the number of syllables in the following line, which you write in your notepad: 'My horse, my horse, will not eat grass'.

Now, highlight the longer sounding syllables and then the shorter sounding syllables in a different colour.

Di dum, di dum, di dum, di dum is a good way of summing this up.

You should then try to write your own lines that match this rhythm. You have one minute to see how many you can write!

Examples include:
'My cheese smells bad because it's hot'
and
'I do not like to write in rhyme'.

For your poem, why don't you try to play with the rhythm? Use only longer beats or shorter beats? Create your own beat and write your lines to this?

Did you know ... ?

Did you know that paper was invented in China around 105AD by Ts'ai Lun. The first English paper mill didn't open until 1590 and was in Dartford.

Rhyme Workshop

Start off with the phrase 'I'd rather be silver than gold' in your notepad. and see if you can come up with lines that rhyme with it -
'I'd rather have hair than be bald'
'I'd rather be young than be old'
'I'd rather be hot than cold'
'I'd rather be bought than sold'

Also, pick one of these words and see how many rhymes you can find:

Rose

Wall

Warm

Danger

What kinds of rhymes did you come up with? Are there differences in rhymes? Do some words rhyme more cleanly than others? Which do you prefer and why?

Lists Workshop

Game - you (and you can ask your friends or family too) to write as many reasons as possible for the following topics:

Annoying things about siblings

The worst pets ever

The most disgusting ingredients for a soup you can think of

Why not try writing a poem with the same first 2, 3 or 4 words?

I am ...

Or

I love it when ...

Eg:

I am a brother

I am a listener

I am a collector of secrets

I am a messer of bedrooms.

Onomatopoeia Workshop

Divide a sheet of A4 paper into 8 squares.

You then have thirty seconds to draw/write what could make the following sounds:

Splash	Ping
Drip	Bang
Rip	Croak
Crack	Splash

Now try writing your own ideas of onomatopoeia. Why might a writer include onomatopoeia in their writing?

Repetition Workshop

Come up with a list of words/ phrases, aim for at least 5. You now must include one of these words in your piece at least 6 times. You aren't allowed to place these words/ phrases at the beginning of any of the lines.

Suggested words/phrases:

Why

Freedom

Laughing

That was the best day ever

I can't find the door

I'm in trouble again

The best

Workshop
POETRY 101

Below is a poem written especially for poetry matters, by MC MiXy.
Why not try and write some more poems of your own?

What is Matter?

© MC Mixy

What matters to me may not be the same things that matter to you
You may not agree with my opinion mentality or attitude
The order in which I line up my priorities to move
Choose to include my view and do what I do due to my mood
And state of mind
I make the time to place the lines on stacks of paper and binds
Concentrate on my artwork hard I can't just pass and scrape behind
Always keep close mates of mine that make things right
And even those who can't … just cos I love the way they can try
What matters to me is doing things the right way
It's tough this game of life we play what we think might stray from what
others might say
In this world of individuality we all wanna bring originality
Live life and drift through casually but the vicious reality is
Creativity is unique
Opinions will always differ but if you figure you know the truth, speak
So many things matter to me depending on how tragically deep you wanna
go
I know I need to defy gravity on this balance beam
As I laugh and breathe draft and read map the scene practise piece smash
the beat and graphic release
Visual and vocal it's a standard procedure
Have to believe and don't bite the hand when it feeds ya

If you wanna be a leader you need to stay out of the pen where the sheep
are
The things that matter to me are
My art and my friends
That will stay from the start to the end
People will do things you find hard to amend
Expect the attacks and prepare you gotta be smart to defend
I put my whole heart in the blend the mass is halved yet again
I'm marked by my pen a big fish fighting sharks of men
In a small pond
Dodging harpoons and nets hooks and predators tryna dismember ya
I won't let them I won't get disheartened I can fend for myself
As long as I'm doing what's important
I'm my mind where I'm supported is a just cause to be supporting
In these appalling hard times I often find myself falling when
Only two aspects of my life keep me sane and allow me to stand tall again
Out of all of them two is a small number
It's a reminder I remind ya to hold necessity and let luxury fall under
Try to avoid letting depression seep through
Take the lesson we actually need a lot less than we think we do
So what matters to you?
They may be similar to things that matter to me
I'm actually lacking the need of things I feel would help me to succeed
Though I like to keep it simple, I wanna love, I wanna breed
I'm one of many individuals in this world where importance fluctuates and
varies
Things that matter will come and go
But the ones that stay for long enough must be worth keeping close
If you're not sure now don't watch it you'll know when you need to know
Me, I think I know now … yet I feel and fear I don't.

Turn overleaf for a poem by Mark Grist and some fantastic hints and tips!

Workshop
POETRY 101

What Tie Should I Wear Today?

© Mark Grist

I wish I had a tie that was suave and silk and slick,
One with flair, that's debonair and would enchant with just one flick,
Yeah, I'd like that … a tie that's hypnotizing,
I'd be very restrained and avoid womanising,
But all the lady teachers would still say 'Mr Grist your tie's so charming!'
As I cruise into their classrooms with it striking and disarming.
At parents' evenings my tie's charm would suffice,
In getting mums to whisper as they leave 'Your English teacher seems nice!'

Or maybe an evil-looking tie - one that's the business,
Where students will go 'Watch out! Mr Grist is
on the prowl with that evil tie.'
The one that cornered Josh and then ripped out his eye.
Yeah no one ever whispers, no one ever sniggers,
Or my tie would rear up and you'd wet your knickers.
Maybe one girl just hasn't heard the warning,
Cos she overslept and turned up late to school that morning,
And so I'd catch her in my lesson yawning … oh dear.
I'd try to calm it down, but this tie's got bad ideas.
It'd size the girl up and then just as she fears,
Dive in like a serpent snapping at her ears.
There'd be a scream, some blood and lots and lots of tears,
And she wouldn't be able to yawn again for years.

Or maybe … a tie that everyone agrees is mighty fine
And people travel from miles around to gawp at the design
I'd like that … a tie that pushes the boundaries of tieware right up to the limit
It'd make emos wipe their tears away while chavs say 'It's wicked innit?'
and footy lads would stop me with 'I'd wear that if I ever won the cup.'
And I'd walk through Peterborough to slapped backs, high fives, thumbs up
While monosyllabic teenagers would just stand there going 'Yup.'

I don't know. I'd never be sure which of the three to try
As any decision between them would always end a tie.

Tips and Advice for
PERFORMING
Your Poem

So you've written your poem, now how about performing it.
Whether you read your poem for the first time in front of your class, school
or strangers at an open mic event or poetry slam, these tips will help you
make the best of your performance.

Breathe and try to relax.

Every poet that reads in front of people for the first time feels a bit nervous,
when you're there you are in charge and nothing serious can go wrong.

People at poetry slams or readings are there to support the poets. They really are!

**If you can learn your poem off by heart that is brilliant, however having a piece of paper or
notebook with your work in is fine, though try not to hide behind these.**

It's better to get some eye contact with the audience.
If you're nervous find a friendly face to focus on.

Try to read slowly and clearly and enjoy your time in the spotlight.

**Don't rush up to the microphone, make sure it's at the right height for you and if you need
it adjusted ask one of the team around you.**

Before you start, stand up as straight as you can and get your body as
comfortable as you can and remember to hold your head up.

The microphone can only amplify what what's spoken into it; if you're very loud you might
end up deafening people and if you only whisper or stand too far away you won't be heard.

**When you say something before your poem, whether that's hello or just the title of your
poem, try and have a listen to how loud you sound. If you're too quiet move closer to the
microphone, if you're too loud move back a bit.**

Remember to breathe! Don't try to say your poem so quickly you can't find
time to catch your breath.

And finally, **enjoy!**

Poetry FACTS

Here are a selection of fascinating poetry facts!

No word in the English language rhymes with 'MONTH'.

William Shakespeare was born on 23rd April 1564 and died on 23rd April 1616.

The haiku is one of the shortest forms of poetic writing.
Originating in Japan, a haiku poem is only seventeen syllables, typically broken down into three lines of five, seven and five syllables respectively.

**The motto of the Globe Theatre was 'totus mundus agit histrionem'
(the whole world is a playhouse).**

The Children's Laureate award was an idea by Ted Hughes and Michael Morpurgo.

The 25th January each year is Burns' Night, an occasion in honour of Scotland's national poet Robert Burns.

Spike Milligan's 'On the Ning Nang Nong' was voted the UK's favourite comic poem in 1998.

Did you know *onomatopoeia* means the word you use sounds like the word you are describing – like the rain *pitter-patters* or the snow *crunches* under my foot.

'Go' is the shortest complete sentence in the English language.

**Did you know rhymes were used in olden days to help people remember the news?
Ring-o'-roses is about the Plague!**

The Nursery Rhyme 'Old King Cole' is based on a real king and a real historical event. King Cole is supposed to have been an actual monarch of Britain who ruled around 200 A.D.

Edward Lear popularised the limerick with his poem 'The Owl and the Pussy-Cat'.

Lewis Carroll's poem 'The Jabberwocky' is written in nonsense style.

POEM – noun

1. a composition in verse, esp. one that is characterized by a highly developed artistic form and by the use of heightened language and rhythm to express an intensely imaginative interpretation of the subject.

Poetry TIPS

We have compiled some helpful tips for you budding poets...

In order to write poetry, read lots of poetry!

Keep a notebook with you at all times so you can write whenever
(and wherever) inspiration strikes.

Every line of a poem should be important to the poem and interesting to read.
A poem with only 3 great lines should be 3 lines long.

Use an online rhyming dictionary to improve your vocabulary.

Use free workshops and help sheets to learn new poetry styles.

Experiment with visual patterns - does your written poetry create
a good pattern on the page?

Try to create pictures in the reader's mind - aim to fire the imagination.

Develop your voice. Become comfortable with how you write.

Listen to criticism, and try to learn from it, but don't live or die by it.

Say what you want to say, let the reader decide what it means.

Notice what makes other's poetry memorable. Capture it,
mix it up and make it your own. (Don't copy other's work word for word!)

Go wild. Be funny. Be serious. Be whatever you want!

Grab hold of something you feel - anything you feel - and write it.

The more you write, the more you develop. Write poetry often.

Use your imagination, your own way of seeing.

Feel free to write a bad poem, it will develop your 'voice'.

Did you know ...?

'The Epic of Gilgamesh' was written thousands of years ago in
Mesopotamia and is the oldest poem on record.

Wordsmith

The *premier* magazine
for creative young people

A platform for your imagination and creativity. Showcase your ideas and have your say. Welcome to a place where like-minded young people express their personalities and individuality knows no limits.

For further information visit *www.youngwriters.co.uk*.

A peek into Wordsmith world ...

Poetry and Short Stories
We feature both themed and non-themed work every issue. Previous themes have included; dreams and aspirations, superhero stories and ghostly tales.

Next Generation Author
This section devotes two whole pages to one of our readers' work. The perfect place to showcase a selection of your poems, stories or both!

Guest Author Features & Workshops
Interesting and informative tutorials on different styles of poetry and creative writing. Famous authors and illustrators share their advice with us on how to create gripping stories and magical picturebooks. Novelists like Michael Morpurgo and Celia Rees go under the spotlight to answer our questions.

The fun doesn't stop there ...
Every issue we tell you what events are coming up across the country. We keep you up to date with the latest film and book releases and we feature some yummy recipes to help feed the brain and get the creative juices flowing.

So with all this and more, Wordsmith is *the* magazine to be reading.

If you are too young for Wordsmith magazine or have a younger friend who enjoys creative writing, then check out Scribbler!. Scribbler! is for 7-11 year-olds and is jam-packed full of brilliant features, young writers' work, competitions and interviews too. For further information check out *www.youngwriters.co.uk* or ask an adult to call us on (01733) 890066.

To get an adult to subscribe to either magazine for you, ask them to visit the website or give us a call.

Friends

Friends are very special,
Special as can be,
We can see a lot of love in us three.

We are like flying friendship birds,
Flying in the sky,
We fly around the way we walk to help those ones who cry.

We don't leave each other out in anything we do,
We will help each other and you too,
We will go to school together all the way through.

And we will hold hands all the way through those scary moments,
The way all best friends should do.

Rebecca Hulse (12)
Litherland High School, Liverpool

My Love Poem

Love,
Is like a flower,
Growing in a plant pot.

Every day I see my family,
The seed in the plant pot grows,
A little bit every day,
Just like mine and my family's love.

Yes we will have our ups and downs,
But nobody ever falls out,
Because we want the seed to grow,
Into a lovely sunflower.

Katie Seanor (12)
Litherland High School, Liverpool

I Love My Family

I love my family
They are very trustworthy

Every day our love grows
Just like a flower in a flower garden

Families are always there
When you need care

We can be happy
We can be sad
And sometimes we can even be mad

But we will always be a family.

Shannon McManus (12)
Litherland High School, Liverpool

Beer

Beer, beer, beer it makes me burp,
Beer, beer, beer quenches my thirst,
Beer, beer, beer is so very nice,
Beer, beer, beer half price.
I like to drink beer yes I do,
I like to drink that runny brew.
I drink it with ice to keep it cold,
It's so precious to me just like gold.
Beer, it's so nice . . .

Tom Shearer (12)
Litherland High School, Liverpool

Day And Night

Day and night pass me by but what really changes?
Light to dark, dark to light but what is the real difference?

Animals change, birds to bats
But what is the real difference?
People sleep, it's all quiet but what really changes?

Do you know the real difference?
It's all around you but you can't see it can you?
That's the real difference.

Kyle Dickey (13)
Litherland High School, Liverpool

Trust

Trust with someone special
Is like a horse
Strong, majestic, beautiful
It takes years to develop
But it can always fall
At the final hurdle
And sometimes
It can't be restored.

Katy Stopforth (12)
Litherland High School, Liverpool

Family

There are close relatives
Who stay in touch
And there are relatives that do not.

But if you love them it won't matter,
If they're close or not.

Joe Alexander (12)
Litherland High School, Liverpool

Sound

I like sound in rooms.
The laughter of young children.
The singing of the school choir.
The sound of a guitar's strings twang
The sound of a violin in the background.
The popping of bubbles from children of two onwards.

I love sound!

Lucy Madden (11)
Litherland High School, Liverpool

Eyes

In your brown eyes,
You made me cry,
In your blue eyes,
You watched me go,
In your green eyes,
You called my bluff,
You watched me leave now it's tough.

Holly Tulloch (13)
Litherland High School, Liverpool

My Grandad

My grandad was a treasure to me
A gentleman is what people see
My nan was a twinkle in his eye
The girl with the golden legs,
He'd say as she walked on by.

Emma Beard (12)
Litherland High School, Liverpool

Trust

Trust is like a shoelace
You can tie it and untie it,
You can play with it
You can open it up,
Once you've tied it never let go.

Andrew Wright
Litherland High School, Liverpool

A Typical Day

I woke up in the morning and hit my head
My dog was barking, his name is Fred
He barked and barked until I got up
I was bleeding so much it filled a cup
My mum was shouting up into my room
'Come on sweetie, we're leaving soon'
I got in the car, put my belt on
'Have you got any homework?'
'No Mum I have none'
I got into school, got on with work
At break time I went for a lurk
My science was difficult, we were doing magnets
I was told to get them from the cabinets
Next lesson was easy, it was French
In PE I was made to sit on the bench
After school, I ran as fast as I can
I saw my dad in his white van
He pulled up and gave me a ride
He told me, 'Son, you will wanna hide.
Your mate is coming around
He'll be seeking and soon you will be found'
After that I went to bed
And I whispered, 'Goodnight Fred.'

Brodie Mulvaney (12)
Marden Bridge Middle School, Whitley Bay

Cassie Matters To Me

Because she is

Adorable
When she has just woken
And not fully awake
She looks just like a puppy again

Because she is

Friendly
She just wants to be everyone's friend
When she sees you
She doesn't attack you

Because she is

Wrinkly
All British bulldogs are
Snow coloured wrinkles
She blends into the snow

Because she is

A thief
Steals socks and underwear
Rips them and takes them in the garden
With towels and tea towels

Because she is

Mental
When she has mental moments
Running into things for no reason
Running around the house and garden.

Ross Parker (12)
Marden Bridge Middle School, Whitley Bay

Shopaholic

Look through the window,
With your eyes twinkling.
Waiting for the door to open,
With your cash jingling.

You hear a creak,
Is the window breaking?
No, wait a moment,
It's the door opening.

You run as fast as you can,
You pick something you like.
After a few seconds,
You feel like you've been on a hike.

You see a pair of leather boots,
A heavenly light appears.
A couple of seconds later,
They both disappear.

You make a run for it,
You see them with a girl.
You give a big nudge,
5 minutes later the room gives a twirl.

The girl screams,
You run with the boots.
Next thing you know,
You're outside giving a loud hoot!

Monika Hussain (12)
Marden Bridge Middle School, Whitley Bay

My Sport

What matters to me
My sport
Rugby in fact
It's tough, hard and it's fun
It's fast
I play with my friends
We win
Or we lose
I get inspiration from older players
Like Kevin Sinfield
Or Rob Burrow
I love sport so much
I do mountain biking
It's fast
It's fun
As you dodge the trees and the rocks
And you get lots of speed on the hill
It's also hard as well
But you need skill
Like older riders
Like Sam Pilgrim
And Scott Craner
They are the best to me
If I was as good as them
I would be a champion
And that is what matters to me.

Aidan McCallion (12)
Marden Bridge Middle School, Whitley Bay

The Big Match

Whoop! The whistle blows,
Where's the ball going next? Nobody knows,
Hits a foot and it's on the wing,
Hear their fans starting to sing,
Cross the ball where's it going?
Look in the sky it's started snowing,
Header! Header! We know it's wet,
Make sure the ball's in the back of the net,
Referee, referee come on that's definitely a penalty!
Get the ball on the spot,
Make sure the players are outside the box,
Put that foot through the ball,
Yes, yes what a goal.
That's the end, the fans are leaving,
Outside the stadium the fans are heaving.
Come on now get to the bus,
The away fans have had enough.

Jordan Ellis (13)
Marden Bridge Middle School, Whitley Bay

London 2012

Bang, bang goes the gun
Athletic runners who have won
Usain Bolt on the run
Lots of fans having fun
Halfway through now it's on
Usain Bolt is the only one
A British man comes through
Fans don't know what to do
Heads down past the line
Celebrations with food and wine
Usain Bolt may have won
But the British man deserves a well done.

Andrew West (12)
Marden Bridge Middle School, Whitley Bay

Trampolines

Trampolines are bouncy
You bounce on them all day
If you see an elephant
The springs will break away
If you see a spider
It will dangle down the holes
If you see a person
They will flip, flop, drop all around
If you bounce so, so high
You will rocket to the sky
I love trampolines
They are the best
If you are bored, jump on one
If you don't have one
Hop to the next-door neighbour's
If you are good enough
Spring to the Olympics in 2012.

Sarah Amy Willox (12)
Marden Bridge Middle School, Whitley Bay

Writing About Me

I am a slow slug in the morning
My eyes are sparkling crystals
My hair is a curly sheep's coat
My arms are cold icicles
Hanging off roofs
My mind is alarm bells ringing
And never stops
My head is a blown-up balloon
Floating on a stick
My legs are floppy sausages
My mouth is a television
Babbling on.

Amie Knox (12)
Marden Bridge Middle School, Whitley Bay

Insects

Twenty spiders climbed up a wall,
Eighteen spiders had a bad fall,
The rest had collapsed,
Whilst they ran two laps,
And got squashed by a bag of coal.

Twenty beetles crawled up a log,
Seventeen beetles had a bog,
They had a wee-wee,
Before their tea-tea,
But got eaten by a big dog.

Twenty caterpillars crawled off,
Whilst ten of them started to cough,
They ate a big leaf,
With their blunted teeth,
And their mum was a scary goth.

Mark Wright [12]
Marden Bridge Middle School, Whitley Bay

What Is It?

It is hairy, it is fierce
It has got big ears
It lights up in the darkness
It eats whatever it can find

It's coming closer
What can it be?
You can see its big ears
You can smell its nasty breath

Hungry as a lion it comes closer
What can I expect?
I saw a glimpse of it and finally
It's a bear!

Jordan Harkus [13]
Marden Bridge Middle School, Whitley Bay

Who Am I?

Money maker
Music singer
Clothes modeller
Good dancer

Great career
Group singer
Book writer
Make-up lover

TV presenter
Show judger
Shampoo advertiser
Award winner

Who am I?

Cheryl Cole.

Amie Tate (13)
Marden Bridge Middle School, Whitley Bay

Who's This Man?

X Factor
Pants higher
T-shirt greyer
Charity giver

No nicer
Hairy chester
Career greater
Show judger

Storm hater
More richer
An ITVer
Cher lover.

Abigail Kilmartin (12)
Marden Bridge Middle School, Whitley Bay

A Star!

Dress wearer
Show judger
Boy leader
X Factor lover

Water drinker
Style starter
Perfume producer
Book writer

Award winner
Ethan carer
Harsh commentator
Hair curler

Who am I?

Dannii Minogue

Jessamay Leach (12)
Marden Bridge Middle School, Whitley Bay

Who Am I?

Money maker
High waister
Suit wearer
Hairy chester

Show judger
Harsh commentator
Award winner
Charity giver

Group leader
Storm hater
Bright smiler
American liver.

Robyn Luckley (13)
Marden Bridge Middle School, Whitley Bay

Guess The Star!

High wearer
Show judger
Storm hater
Group leader

X Factor lover
Water drinker
Harsh commentator
Award winner

Money maker
Diva Fever
American liver
Hairy chester

Who am I?

Simon Cowell!

Demi Lathan (12)
Marden Bridge Middle School, Whitley Bay

Jeff Hardy

High diver
Good wrestler
Crazy jumper
Good winner
Crazy dancer
Bright glower
Painful faller
Fast runner
Brilliant respecter
Money maker
Diamond smiler
Party rocker.

Amber Greer (12)
Marden Bridge Middle School, Whitley Bay

Moonlight

Edward lover
Jacob kisser
Lie teller
Truck driver

Bad dreamer
Edward rider
Mind shielder
Volturi hater

Bike rider
Bad dancer
Scribbly writer
Renesmee carrier

Who am I?

Bella Swan - Twilight.

Tyler Crow (12)
Marden Bridge Middle School, Whitley Bay

My Friends!

My friends make me laugh,
My friends make me smile,
My friends are there for me,
They make me have a big smile,
My friends listen to what I have to say,
Where would I be without my friends?

My friends smile,
I smile,
We stick together and don't leave one another,
I'm always there for them.

Paige Elsender (12)
Marden Bridge Middle School, Whitley Bay

What Matters To Me

My life, football

Shooting and scoring
Will never be boring
Passing is easy
But don't be too cheesy.

Attackers are fast, some slow
But don't stop playing
Till the whistle goes.

Defenders defend
Till the end.

Midfielders are in the middle
Some on the wing
They play and play
So the ball will go in.

Joe Greener (13)
Marden Bridge Middle School, Whitley Bay

The Young Toon Lad

There was a young lad from the Toon,
Who played an extremely bad tune,
People ignored him,
When he tried to swim,
The young Toon lad began to 'droon',

No one helped the young drowning lad,
He had already lost his dad,
When the news had come,
His super sad mum,
Started to cry which made her mad.

Thomas Rock (12)
Marden Bridge Middle School, Whitley Bay

Cheryl Cole

Good singer
Great dancer
Fashion weaver
Money taker
Video maker
Chance giver
Hair styler
Make-up wearer
Girl judger
Dimple styler
Ashley hater
Heel wearer
Cool smiler
Geordie talker
Hair dyer

Danielle Hall (12)
Marden Bridge Middle School, Whitley Bay

A Dog's Life

Fast runners
Big eaters
Cat chasers
Bone finders

Dog sniffer
Toy chewer
Nap taker
Water hater

Big smiler
Lead puller
Meat eater
Human lover

What am I?

Simon Stuart (12)
Marden Bridge Middle School, Whitley Bay

Never Forget Me

The sky is blue
Blood is red
When you tell him to
He can't be bothered to get out of bed.

He said that he would go to the shops but
He must have come to a stop
He must have had a late night
Because he said he doesn't feel right.

Feeling weary as can be
He said come here to me
I came to him and said
'What is going on in your head?'
He touched my shoulder and knelt on his knee
'Never forget me.'

Daniel O'Neill (12)
Marden Bridge Middle School, Whitley Bay

We Want Our Teachers Back

In school today we had a surprise,
No usual teachers, all supplies,
Each teacher was a dinosaur,
Not a person to ignore,
The diplodocus began to focus on scientific hocus-pocus,
The brontosaurus taught us a chorus from his enormous thesaurus,
The archaptrix taught us flying from one fifteen to half-past six,
The megaraptor read us a chapter from some dull book,
It really grabbed her,
The iguanodon went on and on a mad mathematical marathon,
I hope these monsters disappear,
Can't stand this dreadful stuff all year,
We want our normal teachers back,
Please give these creatures all the sack.

Abdul Nadeem (12)
Marden Bridge Middle School, Whitley Bay

The Old Lady

An old lady stood in the light,
She got a big fright one cold night,
She fell on the floor,
And cried for no more,
Then something walked into the light.

The figure disappeared quickly,
The lady stood up suddenly,
She ran out the door,
And fell to the floor,
She then faded away . . . scary!

Holly Stothert (12)
Marden Bridge Middle School, Whitley Bay

I Am . . .

I wake up, I am a sloth.
My hair is an incomplete jigsaw.
My mind is a fried egg.
I am an elephant, going down the stairs.
My mouth is an overflowing waterfall,
My smile is an upside-down rainbow.
I am a hedgehog in the car.
I am a bull, charging down the road.
I see my friends, I am a hyena.

Erin Charlton (12)
Marden Bridge Middle School, Whitley Bay

My Mysterious Body

My heart is a ticking time bomb
My mouth is a hungry crocodile
When I am playing hide-and-seek I am a ghost
When I am playing football I am a ninja
My hair is an ever growing tree
I am an old cat in the mornings
When I watch the TV I am a zombie
My mind is an office computer always working
When I walk down the stairs I am an elephant.

Lewis Fox (12)
Marden Bridge Middle School, Whitley Bay

My Grandad

It broke our hearts to lose you
But you didn't go alone
A part of us went with you
The day you left home

A million times we missed you
A million times we cried
If love could have saved you
You never would have died.

Georgina Little (12)
Marden Bridge Middle School, Whitley Bay

My Life

I know you have Odball and Lucky
And Nana Florrie too
All our love and memories
Are still with you. We miss you.

Rachael Sanderson (12)
Marden Bridge Middle School, Whitley Bay

I Am

I am a hungry crocodile,
My hair is a spiky hedgehog,
In goal I am an eagle swooping on its prey,
My mind is a calm sea.
At night I am a monkey swinging round the house.
I am a tiger ready to pounce,
My tongue is a slippery snake,
My brain is an alarm clock never stopping.

Allan Lopez (12)
Marden Bridge Middle School, Whitley Bay

Skate Or Die

There we go what a kickflip,
Up the quarter that's a tailwhip,
Smashin', crashin', grindin' my bones,
All you'll hear is moans and groans,
Ridin' my bike, skating the road,
180 barspin, what a show,
To the skate park, what a place to go,
Ridin' street I go solo.

Calum Gray (12)
Marden Bridge Middle School, Whitley Bay

My Family

What is important to me is my family
I like to sit at home while they give me tea
I like it how the whole house revolves around me
This poem it's not true, it's just to entertain you.

Robbie Brand (12)
Marden Bridge Middle School, Whitley Bay

Metaphor

In the morning I am a butterfly fluttering around.
My hair is a spring on a trampoline.
In dance I am a graceful swan dancing about.
My mind is a goldfish
My eyes are a swimming pool floating about
My legs are kangaroos
My fingers are clickey pens
My stare is a glowing light bulb.

Shantelle Wallis (12)
Marden Bridge Middle School, Whitley Bay

Birds

There are different species.
Different kinds of birds.
Most birds are herbivores.
And some are carnivores.
They are protected by the RSPB
Some are harmless.
But most are vicious.
All birds are beautiful.

Lee Sheavils (12)
Marden Bridge Middle School, Whitley Bay

Tongue Twister

Funny frog falling fast through the forest
Weird worm wiggling wildly round the world
Dirty dog dancing during drama lesson
Crying cat eating cream cakes
Slow swans swimming while singing songs in the sunset
Silly snails slithering sideways singing a silly song.
Hungry hen hatching a handful of heaven.

Ethan Colley (12)
Marden Bridge Middle School, Whitley Bay

My Friends

What matters to me
Are my friends
They're kind, fun and laughable
They love me and I do too
They're cool, caring and the best
But they matter to me
And they always will.

Rebecca Toogood (12)
Marden Bridge Middle School, Whitley Bay

What Matters To Me

My family matters to me
They are my whole heart
I love and trust my family
There may be an argument
Once in a while
But that just brings us
Closer together.

Levi Robinson (12)
Marden Bridge Middle School, Whitley Bay

Sun Burning

Bushes waving side to side,
Grass twitching,
Wind whooshing,
Leaves falling,
Dropping like a waterfall.

Rubbish rolling,
Flowers falling,
Water dripping,
Sun shining,
Birds flying over our heads
Like you're on holiday.
Dogs yelping at the window,
Speeding cars,
Graves shining,
Clouds brightening,
Bins rolling like a car.

Sun reflecting through the windows,
Plants growing,
Shadows moving on the floor.

Hearing thunder,
Rain pouring,
People shocked,
Trees falling,
People falling,
Clouds moving,
Hearing bouncing,
Branches falling,
Wind blowing,
Things glowing
Sun burning.

Britney McCann
MCMA - Girls, Moston

Child Abuse

I sit in my room and get beat every day,
But I think it might stop today.
I lie on my bed crying to myself
I don't know what to do, I can't scream for help.

My dad comes in with a belt,
It's like my heart begins to melt,
I thought my dad was meant to love me.
Please, can you set me free?

I'm surprised they will let me live,
I haven't got simply a toy to play with,
I can't believe they find this fun.
I wish I could talk to my mum.

I feel like I want to run away,
I think I might do that today.
I pack my bags and throw away the key,
Then at least they might love me.

When they find me to hit me again
Or buy me a present - it will probably be a book - 1-10
Or probably nothing - zero = none
They probably haven't noticed that I have gone.

Ayesha Jones & Hayley Smith (13)
MCMA - Girls, Moston

Geek

I get As and Bs but never Cs
I answer every question in all my classes.
Everyone calls me 'Geek',
As they choke in laughter.
But one day they will choke with disasters
In their coming future.

Just because I
Don't wear the latest trends and make-up
I only wear my glasses and my appropriate clothes,
I'm considered a 'low-life geek'.

My life is going pretty high. I'm sure they're the ones
Heading for the 'Low'. One day I'm going to be on TV
Winning a prize for my genius head . . .

I laugh to myself, 'Do they even know what 'Geek' means?
At least I don't get Fs, Es and Ds. Well at least I'm not a 'FED'
At least I've got a definition for that word -
'Failure, Empty, Dummies'
I'm a 'Geek', sure I am a
'Genius, Excellent, Educated, Kid'
So you 'C', being a 'Geek' isn't a bad thing.

Thandeka Moyo
MCMA - Girls, Moston

My Big Boat

I live on a boat - a very big boat,
A very big boat to me!

I sail my boat around a small sea,
A very small sea to me!

My boat is my home, my castle, my palace,
A castle, a palace to me!

Turns out, my boat's small,
My boat's very small,
But my boat is not small to me!

Turns out the sea's big,
The sea's very big,
But the sea is not big to me!

My boat is not big,
I know that now,
My boat is not big, I know!

But my boat's big enough for me!

Emma Barry (14)
MCMA - Girls, Moston

The Mystery Owl

Mops look like broomsticks
With me riding high
Flowers grow green fingers
That colour away the sky.

Look at the night creatures
Peeking through the door
The noise fades slowly
Like a ghost-empty roar.

The glitter mixes moondust
From the sky dropping it below
Light fairies come on the earth
Guided by their glow.

The fairies gather wishes
As a fox starts to howl
All watches by the distance
Of a mysterious looking owl.

Khadeeja Khan
MCMA - Girls, Moston

My Dad - Always Hurting Himself

My dad always seems to hurt himself -
He will come back and moan about his health.

Just the other day he fell off his motorbike
He said he flew through the air,
Without a care -
And he ended up on the floor down there!

He seems to be in a lot of pain,
But I bet he will go back and do it all again!

My dad always seems to be hurting himself -
Even though it's bad for his health!

Rhianne Elliott
MCMA - Girls, Moston

Every Thorn Has A Rose

Every thorn has a rose, just like I have you,
If you weren't here, I don't know what I'd do.

Sometimes I feel like we were just meant to be,
Friends forever and close for eternity.

Our friendship means the world to me,
I'm so happy to have you three.

When I am ill and under the weather,
You are always there to make me better.

I have had rough times throughout my life,
And you've all been there to help me through my troubles and strife.

I could not have asked for more,
As I have three fantastic friends that I absolutely adore.

Sania Choudhry
MCMA - Girls, Moston

Global Warming

The heat is risin'
Come on, let's keep tryin'
Ice caps are melting
We need everyone helping
Time's ticking away
Help us today
We all know it needs sayin'
No good just prayin'
Don't just leave it
We can still save it
It's our home, so let's take care of it
Stop global warming
It's our last warning
Last chance now
We all know how.

Stephanie Douglas (13)
Monkseaton High School, Whitley Bay

The Beatles

The Beatles were from Liverpool,
They went far and wide,
Many thought that they were cool
And they started to guide.

Fans back in '63,
Thought that they were great,
Coming soon was going to be,
The first movie that they made.

Then it got to '64,
Fans were all so loyal,
They got Brian Epstein at their door
And a visit from the Royals!

Turning into '65,
It showed what they could do,
They soon started going 'off' live,
And upsetting more than few.

From '66 to '69,
Many new albums came out,
For they were having a great time,
But drugs caused the fans to shout.

And then in 1970,
The band began to split and shout,
For the last album 'Let It Be',
Guaranteed that they'd be out.

The Beatles were from Liverpool,
They went far and wide,
Many thought that they were cool,
Even at the end of their stride.

Josh Oxley (13)
Monkseaton High School, Whitley Bay

Little Birds

Two little birds
Sit on the big willow tree,
He sings of life,
She sings of love.

They are but a pair
Of friendly smiles.
Beneath branches their shadows meet
And dance with the leaves.
But soon winter will come,
Two little birds must fly away.

Two little birds
Sit on the weeping willow tree.
He sings of anger,
She sings of heartbreak.

Winter makes the tree turn bare,
Two little birds sit apart.
Then he flies away.
In the pond her reflection is broken,
Like her.

One little bird
Sits on the dead willow tree.
He has found another,
She will sing no more.

Hannah Potter (15)
Monkseaton High School, Whitley Bay

Untitled

This is what matters to me
My family
Mam, Dad, whoever they are,
You should love them.

This is what matters to me
Germany
Like, dislike,
I will always love it.

This is what matters to me,
My Xbox,
Broken or working,
I will always love it.

This is what matters to me,
Climbing,
Scared of heights or not,
I will always love it.

This is what matters to me,
Whitley Bay FC,
Fun or not,
I will always love them.

This is me,
Chris Smith.

Chris Smith
Monkseaton High School, Whitley Bay

Family

Family is my whole life
Family are the people who care for me
Family are the people that protect me
Family are the people that treat me
Family is the thing you can only have once.

Amy Murphy (13)
Monkseaton High School, Whitley Bay

122

The Poochie

When we got the poochie,
I was twelve.
She started off as Jossie,
But we named her Gem
From my mam's love of gems
And my stepdad's love of Gemma Atkins.
But we have always loved her,
As she runs down the beach
With her golden fur.
That golden Lab mix chases
The dogs in the sea
And the seaweed sticks we throw,
Until we head off home
To the couchie,
Where we have our sea heads up,
Until we look up
To the Zzzs.
But we still love our poochie,
Even with her love of seaweed
And chasing dogs.
We still love the poochie
And that's my golden beauty.

Michael Crosby
Monkseaton High School, Whitley Bay

Chickens

Chickens, chickens everywhere
Chickens have got hair
They live on a farm
In a woody barn
They wait nice and calm
I wish I lived on a farm.

Ryan Marley (13)
Monkseaton High School, Whitley Bay

My Family

I really love my family,
I care about them so much,
When we're together it makes me smile.
And talk and laugh and such.

First of all there's Mam,
Who taught me all I know,
She makes me happy most of the time,
Especially when I'm low.

My dad does not live with me,
Though I really wish he did,
He's funny, caring, with no hair on his head,
But I'm glad that I'm his kid.

Nana, Nana, the maddest of them all,
Oh, the things that she says,
She really is the best nana in the world,
I hope she stays that way.

Last but not least is Granda,
Who sadly passed away,
I miss him more than you could ever think,
But in my heart he will forever stay.

Millie Dixon (13)
Monkseaton High School, Whitley Bay

Basketball

Every Friday, every Monday,
Every free day, every Sunday,
I am out on the courts,
Playing what's my favourite sport,
One hour, two hours, maybe even three,
Rain, sun or fog but not in the wind.

Andy Ross
Monkseaton High School, Whitley Bay

Untitled

The lie is not shy
But the lie is very sly
The lie likes to make people cry
The lie cannot fly
But the lie can jump very high
Do you lie . . . ?

Would you like to make people cry?
Now would you like to be sly?
But not being able to fly?
And being able to jump very high?
Would you like to tell the lie . . . ?

How would you like it if . . .
Someone was to make you cry
And made a lie that was sly?

Tell the truth, you'll be OK
But tell the lie and you'll regret that day
Honesty isn't just a play
That's all I have to say.

Sophie Grant
Monkseaton High School, Whitley Bay

Sing

I love to sing
I like to make hearts go ping
It's not just a hobby, it's my life
I try and sing even through my strife
One thing I hope is that when I'm old
I want to stand out, I want to be bold
Maybe one day when I walk down the street
I'll be the one people want to meet
But up until then I'll sing my heart out
And I'll stand by the mirror and practise my pout!

Jade-Louise Lumsden-Barker (13)
Monkseaton High School, Whitley Bay

Acceleration

When I clip the board to my feet,
I feel like one of the elite.
At the top of the hill,
That's where many people write their will.
I start going down the hill, oh what a thrill!
There's a number of deaths caused by this sport,
Many people keep appearing in court.
While going down the slope,
All I can do is pray and hope.
The adrenalin running through my veins,
I have surely been let off my reins.
Skidding through the snow,
Oh boy, here I go,
Reaching extreme speeds,
Someone has let me off my lead.
There can only be one name for this sport,
It's the one that beats the rest,
It really is the best,
It is snowboarding.

Lewis Kirkpatrick (13)
Monkseaton High School, Whitley Bay

Friends' Love

Help ever
 Hurt never
Love ever
 Hate never
Give ever
 Expect never
Smile ever
 Cry never
Think friends ever
 Forget friends never.

Farha Islam (14)
Monkseaton High School, Whitley Bay

People

People, people everywhere,
Some are fair
And some don't care.
Some are funny
And some have money,
People, people everywhere.

People, people all around,
Some are bound
And some are round.
Some are small
And some are tall,
People, people all around.

People, people in my head,
People, people go to bed.
Some are caring,
Some like sharing.
People, people in my head,
People, people that are dead.

Jack Taylor (13)
Monkseaton High School, Whitley Bay

Junk Food

Fast food, fast food brings me peace,
Cheesy, cheesy, cheesy crease,
Nuggets, fries, beefburger surprise,
Fast food, fast food brings me peace.

On my perfect dinner plate,
These things would be really great,
Bacon, sausage, eggs and chips,
Fast food, fast food brings me peace.

Billy Bolt (13)
Monkseaton High School, Whitley Bay

When I Said Bye

I sit in the corner of the room,
Crying, crying into my arms,
Calling for Bess, my dog,
Waiting, but she never comes.

I go to look for her,
Shouting, shouting for her to come.
I go to our place and look at her toys,
Crying, crying, then remembering.

I remember, if I shout and wait,
I will be waiting until I die.
I sit in a corner,
Crying, crying into my arms.

I smell the BBQ when I gave her some sausages,
I hear her barking when the postman comes,
I see her sleeping on the bed, but this is my imagination,
Really, she will sleep forever.

George Redfern-Lown (14)
Monkseaton High School, Whitley Bay

Facebook

Status update every hour
Bob Smith is in the shower.
Every second another like
Bob Smith is on his bike.
New profile picture every week
Bob Smith found a spider, eek!
Another comment every day
Bob Smith is running away!
Facebook on my laptop
Facebook on my phone
One more notification
And I'm gonna moan.

Sophie Dunn (13)
Monkseaton High School, Whitley Bay

128

Global Warming

People waste their breath on global warming
But anyone can see
It has no effect at all on you and me!

The Earth's temperature is meant to change
That is a well-known fact
So why do people bother us with all this
Annoying chat?

Look back at history
And how times have changed
We've had ice ages and heatwaves
Over and over again!

So global warming is just a myth
It's so plain to see
That they're just lying to you and me
To try to make loads of money!

Gareth Rowley
Monkseaton High School, Whitley Bay

Family Matters

Why do you care for me?
Why do you buy everything for me?
Why do you stay strong for me?
Why are you always there for me?
Why do you work hard for me?
Is it because you love me?

Why am I grateful to you?
Why can I talk to you?
Why do I say thank you?
Why do I admire you?
Why do I hug you?
It's because I love you.

Eva Butler (15)
Monkseaton High School, Whitley Bay

Bullies

Fat, thin, short, ugly,
Words can make you feel quite lonely.
Just one word can make you cry,
You spend hours wondering why.
Bullies are nobodies and hate it that way,
So they come over and have their say.

They might punch and kick you
Or they might call you thick,
But what they're doing really is sick.
So tell a teacher or tell a friend,
Then all your problems will come to an end.

'What goes around comes around,' my mum tells me,
So maybe the bully will finally see.
I'm stronger than them and it just isn't worth it,
I'm a better person and I'm proud to admit it.

Erin Campbell (13)
Monkseaton High School, Whitley Bay

Shopping

Shopping, shopping, it is fun
I will shop till the day is done
We go shopping to buy things
I like buying big, gold rings.

I like buying lots of shoes
Some of them I hardly use
I get lots and lots of dresses
Looking good always impresses.

Chelsea Wilson-Ford
Monkseaton High School, Whitley Bay

The Match

The whistle blows, people shout,
Now I know what it's all about.
The smell of the food fifteen minutes away,
When we score they scream and shout.

Fifteen minutes have come now,
I'm on my way to get the taste of a great hot dog.
Football, football,
The great game.

Dylan Lee Dry (13)
Monkseaton High School, Whitley Bay

The Beach

It's a place that makes me stop and stare
A place where I can think
As the wind blows freely through my hair
The waves fall back and shrink.

My footprints in the sand are there to see
Until the tide claims them back
The clouds that pass by seem to be waving at me
As the water has covered my tracks.

Deborah Harley (16)
Monkseaton High School, Whitley Bay

The Weekend

I love the weekend because it's fun,
The biscuits, the chocolate, I get it all done.
I listen to music through the night,
It's very relaxing but sometimes a fright.
I love the weekend because it's great,
Mainly because I stay up too late.

Chris Brown (13)
Monkseaton High School, Whitley Bay

What Matters To Me?

It's my life because it is what made me, me.
I am not just a she, I am Bethany.
It's not just my life, it is my family!
These are the things that matter the most to me.
There's my mum, my dad, my brother and my Kitty.
I have a lot of pets.

My auntie had a horse, but I classed it as my own.
I've had a fish who's first name was Clown.
I've had a dog and now I have got a cat
And we come to the end of that.
That's what matters to me the most.

Bethany Johnston (11)
Newall Green High School, Manchester

What Matters To Me?

There's a lot that matters to me,
Maybe a cup of tea!
But others are more important,
Like my amazing family.

They're always there when I need them,
They give me a place to sleep.
They give me food and water
And they help me when I'm hurt.

But there's more than just my family,
I have my friends as well.
They talk to me when I'm lonely
And entertain me all day through.

Not forgetting my hobbies,
Dancing is the best,
But there is also Guides and Scouts
Which stop me sitting on the couch.

My favourite place is my room,
I will never touch a broom!
I love listening to music and I always eat my food.

There's just one more thing to say,
My favourite subject is science
Because it's fun and experimental,
Like me!

Finally, my name is Lauren
And thanks for listening to me.

Lauren Parry (11)
Newall Green High School, Manchester

I Wish

I wish my house was made of chocolate,
I wish that I could fly to the moon,
I wish my mum wouldn't nag so much,
I wish sweets wouldn't cost a lot,
I wish my car had wings like a bird,
So it put me in the sky where I am so high,
I wish this poem would end soon
Because I feel like a right blooming goon!

Alana Hedges (11)
Newall Green High School, Manchester

Love

Behold - two swans.
Ten houseboats on the shore side.
A cyclist on the towpath.
Gentle rain.
Two pigeons in a white apple blossom tree
And through the marsh, the rumble of a train.

Two courting geese waddle on the bank, croaking.
A man unties his boat.
Police cars howl and whoop: then nothing.

Nothing but silence.
You and I.
You and I together.
Love is all around, do you see how easy love is for you and me?
There is love for swans, pigeons too
And now there is love for me and you.

Karina Bailey McNally (14)
St Ambrose Barlow RC High School, Swinton

Forever

This song is not over,
In my soul it'll stay,
My guitar plays,
My mind still sane,
Now sunset has gone,
Night has come,
This music will keep me alive,
Till the day I die,
Forever

I've been through the rough spots,
Walking alone,
When the water shines and the twilight glows,
My guitar by my side,
My iPod in my ears,
Full blast,
Oblivious to the world,
My dear,
Forever.

This song is not over,
In my soul it'll stay,
My guitar plays,
My mind still sane,
Now sunset has gone,
Night has come,
This music will keep me alive,
Till the day I die,
Forever.

Now I don't know,
What has happened to me.
The tree no longer grows,
From the tiny seed,
The truth now known,
Tears run from my eyes,
But the music will keep me alive,
Till the day I die,
Forever.

This song is not over,
In my soul it'll stay,
My guitar plays,
My mind still sane,
Now sunset has gone,
Night has come,
This music will keep me alive,
Till the day I die,
Forever.

With music my heart will still beat,
My breath will come
And when I'm asleep,
The notes start to run,
Music saved my life so now I sing . . .

This song is not over,
In my soul it'll stay,
My guitar plays,
My mind still sane,
Now sunset has gone,
Night has come,
This music will keep me alive,
Till the day I die,
Forever.

This song is not over,
In my soul it'll stay,
My guitar plays,
My mind still sane,
Now sunset has gone,
Night has come,
This music will keep me alive,
Till the day I die,
Forever

Forever,
Forever.

Martina Rodriguez-Losa (12)
St Ambrose Barlow RC High School, Swinton

Trendy Teachers

Here's an interesting rap,
About our school,
It makes our teachers seem like fools.

The first teacher's Miss Unsworth,
She's the heart and soul of school,
7B think she's really cool!

The next teacher up is Mr Bannon,
He wears one blue and one green striped sock.
If you don't do your homework,
He'll get you in a headlock!

Miss Dickinson is our French teacher,
Watch out boys, forget your pen, it's not a game,
You'll lose easily and get the pink pen of shame.

Mrs Crowe we have for maths,
Don't come into class like you're in a show,
But you can't stop because you dropped your compass
On your toe!

Miss Davies is fifth on the list,
When Miss teaches, the lesson science is fun.
Dissected pig's heart for lunch anyone?

Miss Potter teaches us drama,
At first we all laughed, acting out all of our scenes,
Now it's not so funny,
We're as confident as Lightning McQueen!

Mrs Tomkins teaches 7B for RE,
We know she loves singing,
By the end of the lesson, our ears are ringing!

Last but not least we have Mrs Langridge,
Our great history teacher.
Well ta'ra for now, nice to meet ya!

Maxine Velasco & Rachel Traynor (11)
St Edmund Arrowsmith CFL, Whiston

Random Me

My hobbies are simple
I really like to sing,
I love to have a lollipop
It is a simple thing.

My uncle's hamster's cool
It runs around its wheel,
I went to Knowsley Safari Park
And I saw a baby seal.

I know that it is random
But I want you all to know,
Of course that I am random
It's nearly time to go!

My teaching group is cool
It is very funny,
My auntie's favourite animal
Is a cute bunny.

I've made lost of new friends
Since I've started SEA,
Nearly the end of my poem
Hardly anythin' to say.

I want to keep writin'
But it's near the end,
Oh no, it's really time to go
Now I have to press 'send'.

I think my poem is really good
I think it's really mint,
The time has come to finish off
And send it on to print.

Holly Murden (11)
St Edmund Arrowsmith CFL, Whiston

Number One Teacher

Mrs Redmond is my teacher,
She is very, very smart,
What's that going tick-tock?
It's her golden-edged heart.

She's always there to listen,
To lend a helping hand,
Especially when,
I didn't understand.

She helped me achieve my goals,
Level 5 you see,
She put a lot of work and effort
Into my class and me.

She isn't like a teacher,
She's like a friend to us all,
She's watched us sit side by side,
Whilst we wait in the hall.

We're like best friends,
Mrs Redmond and I,
When I leave for senior school
I think I will cry.

But the tears will dry up,
And soon there will be
Another special pupil,
Waiting just like me.

Chloe Liderth (11)
St Edmund Arrowsmith CFL, Whiston

Things I Like

I really like my friends,
They all wear fashionable trends,
Whether I really like them depends,
I really like my friends.

I really like my money,
I will never spend it on honey.
I get my money from my mummy,
I really like my money.

I really like music,
But I don't like acoustic,
Neither does my uncle Mick,
I really like music.

I really like my dog,
Because he chases all the hedgehogs.
Once he ate a frog,
I really like my dog.

I really like my laptop,
I also like lollipops.
I wouldn't want to be chased by a cop,
I really like my laptop.

I really like my bed,
A place to rest my head.
I've got a bear called Ted,
I really like my bed.

Dylan Carr (11)
St Edmund Arrowsmith CFL, Whiston

Animal Matters

This is for all the hunters out there,
Don't shoot the animals, it's not fair.
Killing the animals can't be right,
And they might just get you in the night.

Look, there are some gorillas making toast,
Up in the hills where they stay the most.
When they're chilling in the mountains,
They like playing in the fountains.
Save the gorillas.

Cheetahs can cheat,
But when they're in the heat,
They cannot cheat.
They can run fast,
But it does not last,
Save the cheetahs.

Tiger, not Tigger,
Tigers can jump,
And they don't have a hump.
Save the tiger,
Not the Tigger.

Giraffes have great laughs,
But they hate having baths
And they're good at maths.
Save the giraffes.

Lewis Hunt-Jones [11]
St Edmund Arrowsmith CFL, Whiston

I Love My Friends Lots

They are my world,
I love my friends lots,
They make me happy when I'm down,
I love my friends,
They help me whenever I get stuck,
I love my friends lots,
They are the funniest people ever,
I love my friends lots,
They are always there for me,
I love my friends lots,
They are the best,
I love my friends lots,
They are hilarious,
I love my friends lots,
They are always lovely to me,
I love my friends lots,
They always make me laugh,
I love my friends lots,
They tell me everything,
I love my friends lots,
They always help me with my problems,
I love my friends lots,
They are fab,
I love my friends lots,
And I wouldn't change them for anything.

Rebecca Lacey (13)
St Edmund Arrowsmith CFL, Whiston

Thank You Dorothy

So what else can I say?
We thank you Dorothy
You've just made this a fantastic day
You've just killed the witch
Now she's lying in a ditch
She can't do anything, even twitch
Now we're so happy because she was so snappy
Now as the mayor
I've got to swear
That's the best display I've seen anywhere
Then your colourless house
Squashed her like a mouse
We're not lying, we saw your house flying
Then the wicked old witch started dying
Now here's a gift from all of us
There's no need to fuss
You're no fool
You've just killed a ghoul
The shoes should fit your feet
And they're definitely a treat
I've given her a shake
And I know she's not awake
We will thank you once and we might thank you twice
But now that the witch is dead, she's as cold as ice.

Sean Rice (11)
St Edmund Arrowsmith CFL, Whiston

My Favourite Things

Puppies are so cute, aww!
Bouncy little thing, woof, woof,
Big, floppy ears,
I just want to hug all of them.
They can hardly walk,
Falling on their backs, so cute,
Struggling back up.

Chocolate is so cool,
Eating it after school,
All day eating,
It should be a rule.

Saturdays and Sundays,
No more school,
I hate Mondays,
But I love the sun rays.

Shops, shops, shops,
I want to have one when I grow up.
What would we do without them?
Not much.
Shoes, shops, clothes,
I love them.

Sally Livesey (11)
St Edmund Arrowsmith CFL, Whiston

What Matters To Me

My family are the best to me
They do everything they can
Help me through the good and bad
Even without a plan

My mum buys me everything
And I don't appreciate it
Shoes and socks to tops and jeans
Always in a size that fits

My dad gives me money
Whenever I need some
He gives me all I want
So I can go out and have some fun.

My nan spoils me rotten
Gives me all I could ever want
Takes me shopping in the day
Then to a fancy restaurant

All in all I can say
My family truly are the best
They're better than anything
And better than all the rest.

Eleanor Tomlinson (13)
St Edmund Arrowsmith CFL, Whiston

Things That Matter To Me!

The things I like are simple,
With a little dimple,
Some of them are here,
But some people might sneer.

First of all is Bubbles,
My hamster who has troubles.
Secondly, my town Prescot,
Oh! And here comes Lescott!

Another thing is animals,
And lots of them are cannibals.
My favourite one without a doubt
Is the hamster so no need to pout!

My family are really nice
And my mum cooks good rice.
My dad is really funny,
While my brother really loves honey!

So they are the things that matter,
To me which is covered in batter.
All these things over all these months
Will all hope they won't be a dunce.

Niamh Peacock (11)
St Edmund Arrowsmith CFL, Whiston

Two-Faced

It's hard to know which friends to trust,
Until they stab you in the back,
They take their knife and twist it in,
There's those qualities that they lack.

They take their time,
Devising their plan,
Whilst causing trouble between friends,
All the while thinking that they can.

They burrow their way in,
Made up that we care,
They're pathetic really,
You won't ever again stop and stare.

When they decide they want us back,
We'll laugh and say no,
You should have thought of that,
Before you decided to go.

My friends know how to make me smile,
It's true,
We'll stick together,
Just like we always do.

Lucy Brabin (13)
St Edmund Arrowsmith CFL, Whiston

The World And I

Diamond droplets against the sky
Which is the darkest velvet void
Accompanied by the giant shining pearl
And standing there is I.

Then the brilliant amber sphere
Rises from the ground
And then begins to light everything around
And standing there is I.

The sea, a never-ending sapphire veil
And the grass a vast emerald sea
And standing in the midst of it
Is the one and only me.

However, life must be the most precious gem of all
But it cannot be possessed
It is the only thing everyone has
And surely it's the best
And standing there in the never-ending story of life
Is I.

Charles Flowers (12)
St Edmund Arrowsmith CFL, Whiston

My Daily Life

I love my dear family, my family love me dear
When I see my little dog, it makes me want to cheer
When I run home from school, I redo my image, I feel so cool
I race to my laptop with my newly changed top
My Facebook is waiting, I should now be debating
There, I'm logged in, I must keep my image with a giant safety pin
Wow, the time's gone quick, it's already 7 o'clock
I hear a tiny knock, my dad is coming in the room
I had better think of something quick
I have got to explain, but now I've got to do the same day again.

Matthew Foxcroft (11)
St Edmund Arrowsmith CFL, Whiston

What Matters To Me

My friends, my sisters, my mum and dad
These are the things that make me glad
My lizards, my dog and even my little sister's rabbit
These are the things that give me a good habit
My future, my ups and downs
All these things mess me around
My grandad and nan, my aunties and uncles too
These are the people who help me through
My life, my way, my future as well
All these things give me hell
Good things are going to happen to me, I can tell
My bad weeks and a rainy day
These are the things that stop me from play
My arguments with my family
These things take away my glee
Fights and heartbreaks
These things make me ache
Having my family by my side
Makes this life a roller coaster ride.

Ciaran Lavender (13)
St Edmund Arrowsmith CFL, Whiston

I Love Music

I love music,
The rhythm and beat,
The tap of my feet.
All the great singers,
The click of my fingers.
The bang of a drum,
Makes my ears numb.
The sweet sound,
That goes round and round.
I love music.

Rebekah Hewitt (13)
St Edmund Arrowsmith CFL, Whiston

Call Of Duty Modern Warfare 2

The Xbox turns on,
I sit on my comfy chair
To play on my COD

I have a good game,
But it still drives me insane
When we lose the game.

People say to me,
Why, oh why are you so good?
Well, why do you think?
It is because I was born to play on this game,
Then they say OK.

I get a no scope
On search and destroy, Highrise
I had a great game.

Now I'm getting off,
I'm starting to get tired.
The Xbox turns off.

Michael Pope (13)
St Edmund Arrowsmith CFL, Whiston

Food, Glorious Food

Jaffa Cakes and prawn cocktail crisps are ace!
I love Galaxy
I stuff my face
From biscuits to cups of tea
Then fish, chips and peas
But good old Sammie took the Milky Way.

We love Haribos
And everybody knows
It's sooo great, yeah!

So we can't tell you what they really are
We can only tell you what they taste like.

Can we pretend there's Magic Stars in the night sky?
Like shooting stars
I could really use a Mars bar right now.

I wanna eat a chocolate bar so bad
Standing next to chewies that are green!

Ellen Wardale & Samuel Wallace (11)
St Edmund Arrowsmith CFL, Whiston

All About Me!

My friends, my family are all important to me,
My mum, my dad, my siblings and me!
I have so many friends, I met them at school,
Both primary and senior, they are all so super cool!
My hobbies are art, designing and fun!
On holidays I love shopping, taking pictures and the sun!
Pictures are important to everyone, mostly to me,
This is because they bring back special memories.
My best friends are so special too,
Lots of hugs and kisses from me to you.
Of course, holidays are the best enjoyments of the year,
With lots of laughs, fun and cheer.
The names of my family are Max, May, Maxey and Maisie,
I know, all our names start with 'M', it's a lil' crazy!
My name's Maxine, if you didn't already know me,
Our names are confusing, not as easy as 1, 2, 3.
I love my friends, they are so precious,
We would never betray each other, even if you paid us!

Maxine Velasco [11]
St Edmund Arrowsmith CFL, Whiston

The Sounds Of Sports

I love the sound of sports
The whistle from the referee
The roar from the crowd
The silence when playing golf
The click of the ball hitting the bat
The bang from the gun starting the race
The national anthem being played when winning a medal
The crunch of the tackle
The ping when the ball hits the post
The vroom of the car race
The bang of the race crash.

Jack Lebby [13]
St Edmund Arrowsmith CFL, Whiston

My Poem About Crazy Things

Gorgeous high-heeled shoes,
Beautiful shoes you will not lose.
I love my music,
But my mum listens to classic.
My iPod is my favourite possession,
Downloading music has no progression.
I absolutely love dance,
There, I always take a chance.

I like my friends more than the world,
When I meet new ones, I have always twirled.
Go home from school eating a chocolate bar,
Eating it at home, even in the car.
I'm always on my laptop and because I'm a girl,
I always shop till I drop!

Bethany Mapley (11)
St Edmund Arrowsmith CFL, Whiston

What I Like

I have so many friends,
My loving family too,
When I'm with my friends,
The fun never ends.

I love going on holiday,
The heat, the sun and fun.
When I'm on holiday,
The fun never ends!

Sweets and cakes and food,
Fizzy drinks too,
Eating sweets and cakes and food,
The fun never ends!

Megan English (11)
St Edmund Arrowsmith CFL, Whiston

What Matters To Me?

Everything matters to me
From my family to my PSP,
My family are so kind and nice
My mum and dad love curry and rice,
My pet dog, Dotty, is all so spotty
And my other pet, Toffee, is the colour of coffee.

All my friends are so funny,
One of them even has a bunny.
Some of my friends are really good at rhyming,
Their advice to me is it's all about the timing.
William Shakespeare was the best poet of his time,
This was because his job was to rhyme.

Anthony Lambe (13)
St Edmund Arrowsmith CFL, Whiston

My Happy Life

These are the things that make me happy,
One of them is from Ndubz called Dappy.
I love Facebook, it's so addictive,
When I'm home from school I'm so predictive.
I'm obsessed with everything to do with army,
Guns, tanks, even a nice old bacon barmy.

Football, it is my life,
Some fans get stabbed with a knife
Because of the passion for their club,
To be honest, it's easier to go to a pub.
They could just play on FIFA 11,
If they're good, it's like being in Heaven.

Cameron Burke (13)
St Edmund Arrowsmith CFL, Whiston

Lunchtime

When you're sat chewing your pen
On your bony chair,
Waiting impatiently,
Staring at the clock,
Twiddling your hair,
Tick-tock goes the clock.

The lecture goes on and the teacher babbles away,
We're bored to death and Sir thinks we're listening anyway.
15 seconds to go and it seems so slow,
Maths still goes on, oh no!

I want to get a good place in the line,
While the sun still shines,
Outside there's a rain cloud crossing the sky,
The teacher's coming and may pass me by.

Doodles and scribbles on the page,
I have no work, well I don't care,
The tick of the clock passing away,
It's actually nearly the end of the day.

Lauren Hinton (14)
Selby High School, Selby

My Teddy

My teddy is soft,
He has a blue nose,
He is a particular sort of teddy,
He is a blue-nosed friend!
He is called Peanuts,
I cannot sleep without him,
I can tell him my secrets and feelings,
I'm always there to comfort him,
And he's there to comfort me!

Emily Bunce (11)
Selby High School, Selby

Fridays

Fridays matter to me,
That feeling of being free!
No more boring maths,
And drawing tiresome graphs.
No more brain-hurting science,
And fiddling with some odd appliance.
No more 'Sort that tie out!'
And grumpy old teachers who have to shout.
No more droning on and on and on . . .

No more waking up before the birds or even before the sun!
Just a peaceful two days of pure and simple fun!
So just as the last bell *brings* . . .
I heave a sigh, with a smile, inside I feel I could sing!
Ah-ha! I smile. School's at its end!
And the weekend is at my fingertips,
A time to laugh, sit, play and spend!

Holly Roberts (14)
Selby High School, Selby

Football

The ball soared into the blue sky.
The striker pushed forward through a crowd of faces.
The goalpost opened its mouth to swallow the ball.
The crowd of faces screamed, 'Goal!'

The goalkeeper grabbed the ball with a sullen face.
He had failed to be the giant that grabs and saves the ball
From going into the white net, like a fisherman
Catching fish at sea.

Jack Pickering (13)
Selby High School, Selby

You're In Love

They say the heart's connected to the brain,
Controls emotions like love, stress and pain.
It's true love, it can make you feel sad,
But it is not always so bad.
Yes love can fade like beauty dies
And you'll never know the hows or whys.
But it can be a happy thing,
With great moments worth treasuring.
Cos love, it lights you up inside,
So hold on tight and let it thrive.
They have your heart cos you're in love,
You pray to Heaven up above.
But you don't have to, you'll be fine,
You'll be with him till the end of time.

Sophie Mapplebeck (14)
Selby High School, Selby

The Roller Coaster

Start
Hands shaking
Belly tingling
Throat's tickling

Middle
Heart racing
Loud screaming
Shock beating

Finish
Relief
Calm down
Heart beating
Throat hurting.

Jessica Mellor Davis (12)
Selby High School, Selby

Weekends

Weekends matter to me,
Because of everything possible to see.
We meet up with friends,
And so we get ready to spend.
As we sit and relax in the glorious sun,
The feeling of fun has only just begun.
As the sun disappears,
Then we start to fear,
As our plans could end soon, oh dear.
As we rush to take cover,
We are still in a flutter.
With so much to see and little time to relax,
The days have passed far too fast.

Amy Buckley (14)
Selby High School, Selby

My Ginger Cat

Look at that cute ginger cat
He's sat on my doormat
He's looking quite fat
Poor little cat
My brother has put on his hat
And is getting his baseball bat
He's going to squash that cat flat
Eww, a rat!
Chase it down, wild cat
Mum's sorting the table mat
Luckily she didn't notice the cat
Chasing the mean rat
Woah! What's that? Mum! It's that small brown bat.

Scarlett Bramwell (13)
Selby High School, Selby

My Parents

P erfect
A mazing
R emarkable
E verything to me
N ever lose you
T errific
S nuggling up with you

Love you mam, dad.

Louis Keany (11)
Selby High School, Selby

My Hairspray

My spray holds me together
Whatever the weather
Holds together every day
In its own unique way

Holds my hair so tight
Looks best in the light
Look at my new hairdo
I would recommend it for you.

Nicole Yates (11)
Selby High School, Selby

Recycling

Put the rubbish in the bin
Do not put your rubbish on the street
If you do the rats will eat it
The smell will be terrible
Please use recycling!

Craig Ripley (12)
Selby High School, Selby

Footy Boots

The boots are awesome,
When you see them,
You'll see shining bright orange.

They are the World Cup 2010 boots,
Nearly every player wears them.
Nike boots!

Rhys Shepherd (11)
Selby High School, Selby

Perfect Food

Perfect food to have all the time
I like eating pizza, it makes me feel fine
Zingy, tangy toppings can't wake me up
Zombie-like, I always find a pizza I can cook
All the meals I love to eat
Smelling pizza is a treat.

Elliot Fuller (13)
Selby High School, Selby

Boredom

Boredom is an easy thing.
It occurs when doing nothing.
You get all tired
Because you didn't get hired
For the job you always wanted.

Lee Newsome
Selby High School, Selby

All Day Long

I play in the crisp white snow with him.
I play in the woods with him.
I play tug of war with him.
But the best thing of all is falling asleep with him.

Euan Forsyth (11)
Selby High School, Selby

Untitled

A single dove flew through the air,
Innocent, easy and free,
Its elegant feathers softly ruffled,
So eager and so gently.

As it glided through the air,
Swiftly above the clouds,
Echoing notes, so high, so sweet,
Singing sweetly out loud.

This peacefulness was shattered soon,
As the lightning threw itself down,
Like Poseidon's trusty trident sword,
Stamping harshly on the ground.

The dove began to quiver,
As the forks came down fast,
Striking the dove on its wing,
Heaven never lasts.

From the days of tranquil harmony,
To the frightening present day,
From those who flew without a care,
To those who are dying in every way.

Elena Lindsey (14)
The Blue Coat School, Liverpool

Rain

I am going to write a poem about rain,
I think that I've got the time,
But I don't really know that much about rain,
And I don't really know how to rhyme.

All that I know about rain is this,
That it always makes people wet,
And that it can make people angry too,
But this is as far as I get.

Perhaps I should start with something classic,
Like 'The rain doth flow on me,'
But I'm not very good at that Shakespeare talk,
I'm really rather trendy, you see.

Would you look at that! I've written a poem,
But it's not really at all about rain,
You could say I've defeated the object,
Would it be wise if I just start again?

Imogen Cooper (13)
The Blue Coat School, Liverpool

A Rainy Day

A rainy day is cold and wet,
A rainy day can leave you upset.

Miserable, mournful and grey,
Oh what a terrible day.

Nothing to play, nothing to do,
Maybe I should try scaring someone by screaming, 'Boo!'

Here comes the sun, ready to shine,
Maybe this day will be fine!

Emma Murphy (11)
The Blue Coat School, Liverpool

162

The Moon

The moon,
An orb, which floats across the velvet sky
As a pearl beneath the timeless waves,
Encompassed as if by a thousand swirling grains of sand,
Glinting down to the dark decay below.

A goddess, elegant, proud, perfect and pure,
For generations you have inspired dreaming minds,
Which unto you have gazed, bewitched,
Pondering your mysterious beauty.

Peering down in her blissful perfection,
Never can a soul be left in hopeless solitude,
For the Earth's precious gem is ever watchful,
A guardian to its careless master.

Once basking in that same light and glory as its silvery companion
The cold, corrupted earth squirms in the dark, murky depths below,
Greens long since lost,
Shrouded in inescapable sorrow, deceit and impurity,
Twisted and contorted by jealousy, conflict and vengeance.

Love fades to hate,
Hearts freeze and harden,
Joy turns to grief
When reality bares its ugly teeth,
Life seems bleak . . .

There, exalted, she shines,
An everlasting beacon of hope,
Evading mortality as he arrives, clad in his wintry cloak,
Leaving trails of mourning and despair in his wake.

In the impossible blackness of a foreboding, clouded night,
The eternal guardian, reflects
Beaming down in silent admiration,
Piercing the vale of chaos,
To see the twinkling darkness of the earth
As it glints back to its pearly companion above.

Josh Burnell (17)
The Queen Katherine School, Kendal

Bottoms Up

12 noon, at the pond.
A lone duck drifts
    On the calm water,
Whilst the family rest, basking in the sun.

A small child looks on,
Curious of the tranquil story
Set beneath the willows.

Amongst the lilies, ripples expand
As frogs -   leap   -   through the steps
Of their joyous dance . . .

And land.

All is silent

And, to the onlooker's surprise
The duck pulls its head back   and   thrusts,
Bottom up,
Head immersed in a sanctuary
Amongst friends

An eyebrow is raised
Mummy told me that's bad manners;
To turn your back on people.

But the curiosity suppresses this consciousness.
The curiosity of the unseen.
Only the imagination can understand.

The duck is again visible, whole
                    Peek-a-boo!
Once again, it dives
What lurks beneath?
                    Always drawing it back
Something to fear?
Or perhaps a precious light, a pearl
                    Or a different world?

The child stares to the sky
    A split second passes
            The trance breaks

Glasses . . . Mummy . . . what?

The child looks back,
                    Silence.
The duck has gone - to a different world?

Frances Butcher (16)
The Queen Katherine School, Kendal

Lion

This is boring, so boring,
Stuck in a glass case
Being looked at.

How I long for the savannah,
The grass between my feet,
The laugh of the hyena
The wind in my mane.
Not here, not now,
Behind a sheet of glass
All stiff and rigid.

The savannah,
My family, all gone
Back into the earth.
The sun on my back
Replaced by light bulbs.
The taste of flesh, raw flesh,
All gone. No taste reaches
My ever-snarling mouth.

There's others too,
Animals of all shapes and sizes,
That yearn for their homes,
Their families, stuck behind glass.
Ghosts of people, their past lives
To be stared at, but no one is interested.
Things so old, underground for millions of years,
To be dug up and looked at; to be uninterested in.

Jack Atkinson (14)
The Queen Katherine School, Kendal

Untitled

Freedom offers us a future,
A blank page ready for spoiling,
The road to tomorrow lies ahead,
Rough and dark, wild and untamed,
The white lines only just keeping us
From crossing the border
Into insanity and destruction.
Sodium lights the night path,
The engine creaking and gurgling.

The next day we wake to
Fresh sounds
New smells.

We drive on and on through sleet and snow,
The glass separates us from the weather.
The steamed interior musty,
Tobacco-stained leather seats
Engulf us in a world of their own.

The gentle hum of the road
Is replaced by the unfriendly growl
Of a Monday morning.
Little do the dreary-eyed drivers know
That a mere hour ago
We were the kings of the road,
Controlling our own speed and direction,
We floated from lane to lane,
Without a care in the world.

But we find ourselves sucked
Into the daylight abyss
Of control and class,
Suddenly walls spring up around us,
Throttling our expressions and emotion,
We are not given a chance.

With the onslaught of city life
Comes the bleep of the traffic lights,
The wail of a siren,
Suddenly not quiet and controlled,

The world is unfriendly.

We are caught upon a freight train,
Unable to control
Our own direction and speed.

Ewan Richardson (15)
The Queen Katherine School, Kendal

The Sea

The sea,
Under a mass of rolling, tumbling grey clouds,
White horses gallop in,
Then break upon a half-moon of white sand.
A ripping, rushing wave
Changes as easily as a human's emotions do,
And then
Under a cornflower sky
The sea remains a mirror, unbroken.

The sea,
Crashing, lashing,
Gently, gracefully,
A gust of wind,
A crash of lightning can change
The sea as easily as a smile lights a crowd.

The sea's a snake,
As slippery and as sly as a snake.
Some days a monster,
Other days as calm and as beautiful
As a flower
Lifting her head to the morning sun.

The sea. It changes for me,
And for you;
Just like us unpredictable people do.

Tabitha Topping (13)
The Queen Katherine School, Kendal

Typewriter

It sat in the corner of my room on a fold-up table.
I, somehow, seemed to easily avoid it; without guilt.
I think it was that it was forever cloaked by shadow;
The sunlight lay everywhere but that one corner
As if it wasn't supposed to be given any attention.
Sometimes I would give it a fleeting glance as I reached over for a pencil
Or my keys as I was leaving.
And I would imagine what it would be like to run my fingers over the keys,
How it would feel to put a sheet in the slot, a blank space waiting for a creative spurt.
But my creativity never surfaced and the typewriter would stay in the corner collecting dust.
I wished I could understand the power of it.
Of words, and how they could affect people.
The whispered wisdom flitting through the machinery,
Just waiting to be caught and formed into strings of sentences,
Prose,
Poetry.
Once I forced myself to sit in front of it.
I waited for inspiration, but it never came.
I lit my pipe and watched the smoke spiral above me, disappearing into nothingness,
I never touched the keys.
So I took it to my nephew's house;
I'd wrapped it in blue paper
And gave it to him for his birthday.
He'll use it.
And in my time of giving
A major gain grows . . . from a minor loss.

Ila Colley (14)
The Queen Katherine School, Kendal

Case Closed

Secluded and still,
Deserted; unplayed and untouched,
Yearned to be a music maker.
In its place
The 6-stringed bowless one steals the show
With its wholesome sound and chestnut glow,
The hands that play it develop and grow,
And the violin is engulfed; case closed.

The case unlocks.
It sits; eagerly awaiting,
Glistening, gleaming, glorious,
A brown so natural,
As if carved
Straight from a tree trunk.

The illusion is shattered
By the hand that touches it,
The notes in mind become a tuneless sound,
The violin is played but, alas, not made,
For these hands lack the talent.
But one can still dream,
However unlikely,
Of the violin and hands becoming a team.

Rosanna Hutchings (17)
The Queen Katherine School, Kendal

A Kingfisher

A blur of blue
    A flash of orange,
Comes darting past our eyes.

A sun-stained leaf,
    A sea of sapphire,
Vanishes behind me as I fly.

A jet of colour,
    A darkened silhouette,
Against the cloudless sky.

I glide,
    I swoop,
        I dive,
Into the depths of the river,
Like a knife.

I skim up,
    Victorious,
A minnow shimmering in my beak.

A blur of blue,
    A flash of orange,
Comes darting past your eyes.

Jo Simpson (13)
The Queen Katherine School, Kendal

The Age Of Childhood

Running down the muddy hillside,
Screaming, laughing as one,
Running through the green meadows,
When life had barely begun.

Playing games and running free,
Oh, when life was simple,
Cutting, sticking, all a mess,
Every smile had a dimple.

Getting paint all over ourselves,
Not having a care in the world,
Dressing up in silly clothes,
As we danced and twirled.

Looking back on all those years,
Those brilliant, wonderful days,
I loved those inspirational times
In, oh, so many ways.

How I loved those days of young,
When everything was good,
How I loved the never-ending age,
The age of childhood.

Bethea Baskerville-Muscutt (13)
The Queen Katherine School, Kendal

Penguin In Morrisons

There is a penguin in Morrisons
Walking around
Making no sound.

He's at the fresh fish counter
Eating all the pike
Wearing some trainers
From Nike.

Tirion Parkman (12)
The Queen Katherine School, Kendal

Clay

Hard weathered antique
The form of the earth has learnt patience, the rocks seeming to speak
From its core arose
A substance lacking completion, like a thorn without the rose
Needed is a stream
Wanted is a spirit helping to mould, to work to a dream
The substance lacks fire
It cannot be alive, but it can have life to admire.

Moist spinning splashing
A second stage of being, mothering hands frantic dashing
Smoothly shaping lines
Ideas and thoughts take form, the nurturing maker refines
Now an entity
Burning into what it was not yester, new identity.

Passed between new hands
Evoking spirit and fire now, and seeing different lands
Yet it does not tire
It was shaped through inspiration, and now it must inspire.

Summer Daisy Coupe (15)
The Queen Katherine School, Kendal

Pebbles

Pebbles, my friend,
As dark as a shadow,
Silhouetted in the moonlight,
Her flowing mane,
Whispering in the breeze,
Galloping,
Galloping,
Galloping across the heathery hillside,
A gentle giant,
Pebbles, my friend.

Hannah Russell (12)
The Queen Katherine School, Kendal

Owl

Behind the glass eyes,
Inside the itchy stuffing,
There's a life,
The lost spark of what once was
A roaring fire.
I have a dead rabbit at my feet,
Yet I'm innocent.
Stuck here in a case full of mirrors.
My reflection painted in the glass,
Screaming silently.
People say
I have piercing eyes . . .
Their eyes cut through me.
Some pitying
Others curious.
Nothing to do
But pace the walls of my imagination.
I'm trapped.

Sian Bentley (12)
The Queen Katherine School, Kendal

My Owl Poem

He sits on a branch,
I watch him stare,
I can see him glare,
He watches me.
When the hand strikes 12,
He twit twit twoooos,
It echoes the land.
I see him jump off the branch,
He flies away,
One day I hope he comes back to stay.

Georgia Thompson (12)
The Queen Katherine School, Kendal

Factor X

Schools of pearl parasites consume,
Media fumigates the living room.
Tune into talent on your TV,
Catch Cowell's coup-de-merde reality.

Thousands thrive on the thrill of their trill,
But deafened am I by the drone of this drill.
Self-expression, under a clichéd duress,
But it's entertainment nevertheless.

My thoughts run vein,
And my blood boils thicker.
If it's too problematic, Sharon?
Let me pull the trigger!

So institute this lunacy,
Lock away reclusively,
And let one thing never be forgotten,
X marks the spot of the rotten.

Marcus Loney-Evans (17)
The Queen Katherine School, Kendal

My Sonnet

Deep red blushes across a leafy face;
Rhythmic storms of fragment colour.
Perhaps a waste of gold and copper, vying for a place
In the transient spectrum of retreating summer.
Though it seems autumn's won the fight,
As the sky bids farewell to the intense blue it once embraced,
Sending its poignant farewell upon its infinite flight
To reach rain-sodden earth, obediently bowing under an enemy too often faced.
However nature's not quite ready to relinquish yet;
The crawling fingers of a sinister winter still being kept away,
While an ethereally reminiscent auburn light keeps beauty safely in the net.
And the inky yellowness of a solstice sun keeping the frost at bay.
Besides it's not all doom and gloom.
There's still the sky's greatest treasure to be unveiled - a rising harvest moon.

Caitlin Law (15)
The Queen Katherine School, Kendal

Cassandra

Within the void of the womb, I loll my head,
The eyes of the fragmented starlets a-flitter,
My mind is a prism that the spectrum has fled,
And merge dark growled evergreen to form autumn bitter.
I sleep now to see the Earth tremble apace,
And fibre wheat jasper atomic betwixt tiger eyes,
Reflexial deprivation, doth mask glitters of space,
And far from the present, your universe files.
This onyx vast dimension between A + B,
One of great many, clarity perceives me,
Cool absence of death, gives life, 'tis a curse.
Though blind am I, eyes equal
The universe was always hers.

Danielle Oliver (15)
The Queen Katherine School, Kendal

Ghosts

Chained,
Constantly in fear
Of more work,
Of stopping.

If we stop, it's forever.
Always trapped, on a tether.

Why me?
All around me
Ghosts of past lives,
Ghosts of lost people.

What did I do
To end up like this?
An empty shell,
That's all my life is.

Faith Rea (13)
The Queen Katherine School, Kendal

Grand Piano

I feel the smooth, wooden surface under my fingertips.
When softly pressed, the ivory keys are like footprints in the snow,
Calm and breathtaking.
Light shimmers off the face of its timber.
The smell is divine, a mixture of wood and resin . . . harmony.
The melody.
A thing of beauty . . . a work of art in itself . . . poetry in motion.
Understand the notes and play the beautiful tune.
Feel the chords run through your body and mind.
Dance to the tune as it fills the atmosphere with emotion.
Blissful, moving, carefree.
On top of the world.
Music is life.
Naturally magnificent.

Emily Humble (12)
The Queen Katherine School, Kendal

Sonnet

As I look out of the window,
I see a beautiful town which continues to grow.
In it, my hometown, there's a part of me,
But some of it, I feel I do not know.

I see autumn, leaves falling, red, gold, brown,
I see summer, the occasional sun,
I see winter, the snowflakes falling down,
And finally I see spring has sprung.

As I look to the fields up on the hill,
I wonder, how long they will stay in view,
Because I know they'll continue to build,
And perhaps spoil the town I once knew.

I hope my grandchildren will one day see,
The view that lies before me.

Kate Fearnyough (14)
The Queen Katherine School, Kendal

Dusk

I love to walk, upon an autumn's dusk,
When air has no great burden of the day.
Yet you would drive a thousand miles here thus,
And give me a golden palace should I say.
The sky so blue that blue's not blue enough,
We talk of what I love, Grandfather's words.
Tumpty-tum and then I chopped his head off,
And you vanish through smoke to other worlds.
If I drive through sunsets or when stars shine,
I could laugh aloud, light headed at dusk.
Your mind is working, it leaves me behind,
And stars twinkling just seem such a fuss.
Buy me out. Dusk's my spirit freed from its box,
Do you remember bats in their tic-tac box?

Mary Ormerod (14)
The Queen Katherine School, Kendal

Chair

There stands her rocking chair, gnarled and lifeless,
Where once she slumbered, now only dust lies;
Her great bulk now but a shadow, or less,
No longer am I greeted with those eyes
Of clearest blue, yet somehow so vacant,
As if the whole world were empty to her.
Now her rugged features are blurred,
I can't recall that shrivelled face,
Nor get over the truth it holds,
Where she is gone I cannot.
As memory fades, so does emotion,
Till one day just a dream - yet her bones rot,
What comfort can be found in that notion?
But it is just a chair, or rugged mat,
By crackling fire, where my grandma sat.

Keziah Baskerville-Muscutt (14)
The Queen Katherine School, Kendal

First Love

Those three little words she craves you to speak,
So simple yet so strong.
She craves your love, it's so unique,
Her love for you is forever strong.
But do you truly love her?
Or is it all just lies?
Outrageous things she has tried to be for you,
She's just not your winning prize.
She may be young and naive,
But she knows what her heart seeks.
So would you just look at her please,
While she stands there and weeps,
Because your name is tattooed all over her heart,
Yet she knows some day you will be apart!

Jenna Roberts (14)
The Queen Katherine School, Kendal

Panther!

Panther,
Moving fast,
Dressed in black,
Ready for a quick attack!
Through the grass,
Slinking slow,
He might strike now,
You never know!
A mouse is a noble prize,
Though he spots a bird through hunting eyes!
Panther,
Here he slumbers,
On the mat,
For he is my pussycat!

Beatrice Hooson (12)
The Queen Katherine School, Kendal

The Alley

Down the town I walk tonight,
Past dark, forbidden alleys,
Then my eyes see something in the alley,
Something black and bathed in blood.

It streaked down the passage,
Should I dare to follow?
My body goes but mind stays back,
Then trapped in a corner I grab a pipe,
And then I see nothing but black.

A body I see, liver cut out,
I look away but not before I see the mutilations
This monster has done,
Now the legacy of Jack the Ripper,
Came to become a new nightmare.

Charlie Thompson (11)
Whitburn CE Academy, Whitburn

Sport Is Fun!

Sport is fun,
Because I like to run.
Darren Bent scored a goal,
And then he did a forwards roll.
Peter Crouch might be tall,
But can he really kick a ball?
Ronaldo makes a fabulous trick,
Can he follow up with a great big kick?

Tennis is hard,
Even on the yard.
So I went and bought,
A magnificent tennis court.
I am healthy and fit,
And I even have a pretty good hit.
I pick up my racquet,
And the crowd cheer, 'Go on whack it.'

Cricket hurts bad,
If you don't wear a pad.
I make a catch,
In every match.
I always chat,
But not with a bat.
Freddie's running on the pitch,
And then he falls down a ditch.

I love sport as much as can be,
And soon you will see me on the TV.

Sophie Jacobson (11)
Whitburn CE Academy, Whitburn

All About Me!

This is me, I'm finally here,
I live in the middle of the Tyne and Wear.
My name is Aimee,
I should have said,
But it was my time to go to bed.
My handwriting is bad, I know that for sure,
Don't ask me a sum cos my maths is so poor.
I have a rabbit called Clive,
He is a lion head,
He sleeps in his hutch or even sometimes in a cosy bed!
I love choco milk, bread and chips,
But the one thing I hate is going on ships.
I have straight brown hair, and hazel eyes
And my head is the shape of a blueberry pie.
Table tennis, tennis, piano and drums,
Those are the hobbies I love more than plums.
My family means a lot to me,
But bye for now, see you soon,
See you in the morning, at night or at noon.

Aimee Lambert (11)
Whitburn CE Academy, Whitburn

Halo Reach

H alo is one of the best Xbox games,
A ll people love the game.
L oads of people buy the game,
O ne of the best games ever.

R each is where it's set,
E ach person protects it.
A ll of Reach is peaceful,
C areful though because . . .
H ere comes the Covenant!

Daniel Gough (12)
Whitburn CE Academy, Whitburn

Creeak!

The mansion door is wide open,
My tall shadow quivers in the moonlight,
I take my first step only hoping,
Creeak!

Shattered glass, razor-sharp and dusty,
Lies scattered waiting to bite my soles,
The stench invades my nostrils, reeking, musty,
Creeak!

The floorboards struggle to carry my weight,
Travelling briskly, not daring to wait,
Beats me - I'm only five stone eight!
Creeak!

A voice, a thunderous clap,
Pierces the silent house,
The director yelling cut,
Boy he shouts loudly,
Eeek!

James Shaw (11)
Whitburn CE Academy, Whitburn

Trees

T rees have many mysteries within them, like the Menoa tree of Du
  Weldenvarden.
R oots that are strong do not wither, nor are they reached by the frost.
E very tree has a dryad who guards it with her life.
E very dryad has a name, like Beach or Ash or Willow.
S ome trees have golden leaves while others might have green but they all
  have the same beauty.

Sarah Rose Mitchell (11)
Whitburn CE Academy, Whitburn

Imagination

In your imagination
Anything could happen
You might go to the circus
And see an elephant shot out
Of a cannon!

You might go to a spooky forest
And get chased by a bear!
You could go to ice cream land
And eat ice cream mountains
And never get banned!

You could fly and wave
At passers-by!
I would go to space
And go anywhere
Faster than anyone's pace
Because in your imagination
You can do anything.

Isaac Joyce (11)
Whitburn CE Academy, Whitburn

My Pets

M y pets are the best
Y oung, old, one guinea pig even bald!

P oodles I have none
E ven have thirteen guinea pigs
T wenty-seven of them.
S wim my fish love to do

Beth Moody (11)
Whitburn CE Academy, Whitburn

33 Miners

33 miners trapped in a cave,
Thinking they're never going to see their families again.
No food and water, thinking they're going to die,
Eventually see a camera which will save their lives.
They applaud, cheer, they're over the moon,
They send a message up saying all 33 are well and in the groove.
On the surface the families are celebrating,
Listening to music after days of feeling devastated.
Underground they're getting used to life,
While the experts are thinking of an idea of getting them out alive.
They come up with a solution, it's brilliant news,
Now all they have to do is send down the Phoenix 2.

Michael Bluff (11)
Whitburn CE Academy, Whitburn

School Opinions

S chool bell goes, everyone sighs but off to class we have to go.
C ome into the class the teacher says and get started on designing stairs.
H omework is important to me, teachers say hand the homework to me.
O ur school is very big so we will need a crane to replace everything big.
O ur school is a Church of England school, we have a nearby church.
L ocker bell goes everyone cheers, off to do my homework everyone says!

Chloe Barton (11)
Whitburn CE Academy, Whitburn

Love

L ovely princess and prince
O nce upon a time
V ery happy
E ver after.

Emma Coombs (11)
Whitburn CE Academy, Whitburn

Young Writers Information

We hope you have enjoyed reading this book - and that you will continue to enjoy it in the coming years.

If you like reading and writing poetry drop us a line, or give us a call, and we'll send you a free information pack.

Alternatively if you would like to order further copies of this book or any of our other titles, then please give us a call or log onto our website at www.youngwriters.co.uk

Young Writers Information
Remus House
Coltsfoot Drive
Peterborough
PE2 9BF
(01733) 890066